The Magic of Momentum

Escape Any Rut. Build Winning Streaks. Use Forward Motion to Change the Trajectory of Your Life.

**By
Stephen Guise**

Blog: stephenguise.com

Book resources: minihabits.com/momentum

Copyright & Disclaimer

The Magic of Momentum by Stephen Guise

Copyright © 2022 Selective Entertainment LLC, All Rights Reserved.

No part of this book may be reproduced in any form, except for brief quotations, without written permission from the author.

The information contained in this book is the opinion of the author and is based on the author's personal experiences and observations. The author does not assume any liability whatsoever for the use of or inability to use any or all information contained in this book, and accepts no responsibility for any loss or damages of any kind that may be incurred by the reader as a result of actions arising from the use of information found in this book. Use this information at your own risk.

The author reserves the right to make any changes he deems necessary to future versions of the publication to ensure its accuracy.

Contents

Preface 1
Introduction: Momentum Isn't Fair 8

Part One
The Four Principles of Human Momentum

> **Principle 1**
> You Are Most Likely to Do What You Just Did 28
> **Principle 2**
> Consistent Action over Time Kills Resistance 38
> **Principle 3**
> Perceived Momentum Is Not Real Momentum 54
> **Principle 4**
> Everything You Do Ripples Exponentially 80
> **Chapter 5**
> Environment, Effort, and Momentum 98

Part Two
Mastering Momentum

> **Chapter 6**
> Reversing Negative Momentum 140
> **Chapter 7**
> Creating Positive Momentum Now 170
> **Chapter 8**
> Sustaining Positive Momentum for Life 198
>
> Other Books by Stephen Guise 232

Book Structure

Preface
The preface explains why this book exists. Then it talks about why we discover our potential rather than reach it.

Introduction
The introduction sets the stage for the four principles of momentum. It covers why momentum isn't fair and touches on the difference between physical and human momentum.

Part One Contains Five Chapters
Part one explores the magic. We're going to thoroughly dissect what momentum means in a human life and, equally important, what it doesn't mean. You will discover that your potential is much greater than it seems, thanks to momentum, the most powerful force to transform or improve your life. You will learn how momentum generates exponential success, whereas most other strategies offer linear, self-limiting success.

Part Two Contains Three Chapters
After reading part one, you're going to be eager to experience the magic of momentum! Part two of *The Magic of Momentum* provides practical and actionable techniques to help you master this powerful force, with useful perspective tips to put you in a momentum-first mindset.

* * *

Throughout the book, I have deposited several "golden nuggets." These are especially valuable pieces of wisdom that I recommend remembering. Sometimes the golden nugget will be a sentence or two. Other times, it will be a whole page. They will be labeled clearly so that you don't miss them.

Enjoy!

Preface

Momentum affects our lives at all times. It's invisible and easy to miss: when negative momentum crashes our lives, we blame other things. When positive momentum lifts us up, we credit other things.

Motivation, willpower, habits, and effort all play a role in how you create, break, or sustain momentum, but none are a better focal point than momentum itself, not even habits. Once you see your actions—not just your habits, but all actions—through the lens of momentum, you will act differently.

I wrote this book for four reasons:

1. Momentum is life's most powerful force, more powerful than any other personal growth concept. It shapes our lives in the short and long term. Momentum is *magical* because its power goes beyond intuition and is too significant to be computed or fully understood.
2. Many authors ignore momentum in the self-help and personal growth space. When mentioned, it is misrepresented and oversimplified. This is in part because how we use the word in casual conversation obfuscates its meaning in life.
3. Momentum is more complex than it seems because of its relationship with time. Behavioral momentum can be stronger or weaker than it appears. Time reveals the truth.

4. Blindness to momentum is detrimental, because it prevents you from fixing root problems and instead makes you focus on symptoms.

There's a lot to discuss. Let's begin with your potential. How high do you think your ceiling is in general and in specific areas? It's almost certainly higher than you think!

What it Means to Discover Your Potential

Potential isn't a number or a single, set thing that each of us has. Rather, potential describes what you *could be* in a specific area if you applied yourself correctly. But while potential is supposed to be a projection of a distant but attainable future, in reality, potential is only known shortly before it's realized.

Seeing your potential is like driving in fog. From the right angle or based on other things you've seen, maybe you catch a glimpse of what's further ahead or correctly guess what's there, but, effectively, you can only see maybe one or two increments beyond your current reach.

Who is most likely to see their potential to become a billionaire? Multi-millionaires, because they are the closest people to that elite level of financial success. Those without a million dollars naturally won't consider their potential to earn a *billion* dollars, with so many milestones between here and there. And yet, every billionaire at one point had less than one million dollars. People who have the potential for a billion dollars rarely see that potential until they are well on their way.

This is the nature of life. We can't typically see our highest potential until we are a relatively small number of visible steps away from it.

Of course there will be people who *say* they're going to be president or make a billion dollars, even if they got a C in political science and have a negative net worth. These people are rare and, frankly, delusional. Their aspirations are unreasonable from a mathematical and practical perspective.

Mathematically speaking, the odds of becoming president or a billionaire are each *hundreds of millions to one*. If you are already a senator, however, your presidential dream odds skyrocket to maybe 1,000 to one.[1] This is why we laugh at a kid saying he wants to be president but take seriously a senator saying the same thing. One of them has proven political potential and isn't too far from the highest level.

Practically speaking, it doesn't make sense to aim for president or a billion dollars before you aim for the necessary preceding steps. To make a billion dollars, you must first make one hundred million dollars; before that, one million dollars; before that, $100,000. As for where you'll ultimately peak, that depends on too many factors to calculate, especially because, as you earn more, your potential to earn more increases.

This is not to crush anyone's dreams or tell people what they can't do, it's to point out the progressive nature of discovering your potential.

Potential isn't just about how high you reach; it's about what you've proven able to do and what you can leverage. It's far more valuable to prove yourself able to earn (and manage) $1 million than to actually have $1 million. The money itself can go away! It can get stolen, spent, or consumed by medical bills. Mike Tyson earned $300 million from boxing, then went bankrupt because he couldn't manage his finances. Others with a small salary may manage it so well that they become wealthy.

What's true of politics and finance is true of every aspect of life: Achievement is more about who you become and the assets you can leverage than any given outcome.

Your Upper Potential Is Hidden

If you believe that your full potential is what you perceive it to be *right now, in this spot,* you are selling yourself short. You can't know until you move. This is because most areas of life are loaded with exponential momentum.

Exercise is tough at first, but once you make it habitual and get in shape, it becomes enjoyable and hard *not* to do. To go from hating exercise to craving it is an exponential change that supercharges your potential in that area. Your finances can skyrocket in time from compound interest (or get crushed by it in the form of debt). As you progress in your career, opportunities may expand to other areas. A star athlete, for example, can land a movie role without demonstrating any acting skill. Whenever you reach a new level, you will see additional layers of your potential.

I want to give you a clear example of how progress is exponential and how that hides your potential. Think about different levels of wealth and how they open up more opportunities. This is not an exhaustive list and it only gives a narrow view of benefits, but it gives you an idea of how each level up helps you see new opportunities and thrive in new ways.

1. **Food and shelter security:** At this level of wealth, you don't have to worry about being able to pay rent and buy food. It removes stress and allows you to focus on higher level goals that you might neglect otherwise.
2. **Medical security:** Being able to access and afford primary and emergency medical care is a big level up. This will improve your health and quality of life. It can even save your life if disease is caught early.
3. **Quality of life luxuries:** Massages, float tanks, and

therapists can ensure your mental health and stress levels stay under control. Without these, I would have constant upper back discomfort and pain.

4. **Personal chef/trainer:** A personal chef saves you a lot of time and rescues you from the health consequences of eating too much take-out food. A personal trainer gives you accountability, custom workouts, and external discipline, helping you achieve your fitness goals without requiring as much planning, self-discipline, and management. Both are massive time savers and health boosters. Better health and more free time open possibilities for exploring your dreams and making even more money if you desire.

5. **Private jets, mansions, yachts, extra cars and houses:** If you have this much money, you can do whatever you want and your options are essentially limitless. You even have exclusive investment opportunities. You can do anything from buying an island to changing the world with charitable contributions.

Every breakthrough, whether it's earning more money, gaining more power and influence, gaining competence in a skill, or increasing your self-discipline, changes everything. *Every new level you reach becomes powerful leverage to help you reach higher levels.*

To anyone depressed or down on their luck, to anyone who

wishes their life was different, take note of this phenomenon. In a low state, you can't see *anywhere near* your upper potential. Jim Carrey, Halle Berry, and Sylvester Stallone became movie stars, but did you know that they each were homeless at one point in their lives? Do you think they could see their superstar potential then, when they were worried about shelter and food?

You can't see the true ceiling for your life, only the obstacles above you right now. This is a good thing, because you can bust through what currently looks like your ceiling and create a future that's *much, much better* than what seems possible.

Potential is widely misattributed to things like talent and intelligence. Those things matter, of course, but people overshoot and undershoot their talent and intelligence all the time. Where you end up is based on where and how you move and what assets you pick up (for leverage) along the way.

Introduction: Momentum Isn't Fair

What makes a race fair?

One might say a fair race ensures all participants start at the same time and place. That sounds reasonable. But here's a snapshot of a race that meets those conditions... and it's completely unfair.

All three participants are at the starting line as the starter pistol fires, but they have different states of momentum. Runner A is moving away from the finish line. Runner B is stationary. And finally, Runner C—whom I bet $100 on—already has momentum towards the finish line. This is why you should care about momentum. It makes winning (or losing) easy.

* * *

Before you say this example is unrealistic, I actually won a (swimming) race this way.

The Running Dive

I swam competitively from age six to 18, and one swim meet was at an outdoor pool that had no starting blocks. Competitive swimmers always dive in the water from atop a starting block (except for backstroke, which begins in the water). Without starting blocks at this swim meet, however, we had to dive in from the side of the pool.

When it came time for the team relays, my friend and I noted the unique situation. Beyond the ledge, there were 20 feet of pavement and a grassy area. We had a runway!

Unlike individual races, relay racers in positions 2–4 don't have to wait for a starting sound. They may dive in when their teammate touches the wall. We could anticipate the exact moment to dive in and had no starting block to keep us stationary. Swimmers from the other team loitered near the pool's edge until it was their turn to dive in. We employed a different strategy.

My friend and I waited like aquatic panthers in the grassy area, about 25 feet away from the pool's edge. I was first up, and as my relay mate took her final few strokes, I sprinted towards the edge of the pool, launching myself into the water just as she touched the wall. My friend did the same on his turn.

What a momentum boost! We won the race, and it wasn't close.

Watch any swimming relay and you'll see the swimmers swing their arms before diving just to generate a small amount of forward momentum. In a sport decided by hundredths of a second, that arm swing can be the difference between winning and losing. You can imagine how much a full sprint's worth of momentum helped our team.[1]

Many competitive sports have rules to regulate physical momentum because, if they don't, it can create an unfair advantage. In our lives, momentum plays the same role, significantly helping or hurting us. We must manage our momentum to excel (and prevent downward spirals). As we do, we will notice something that every person should be taught while young.

Life will always be and feel unfair because of momentum.

Physical vs Human Momentum

Oxford Languages dictionary defines momentum as:[2]

1. (Physics) the quantity of motion of a moving body, measured as a product of its mass and velocity.
2. the impetus gained by a moving object. (Impetus means *force of movement*.)

This book is about behavioral, human momentum, which makes the second definition more relevant. We want to know how long we can keep doing good things for our lives, and the second definition speaks of the *force of movement*, which influences how long momentum will last. What's the "force" of an action? Does one type of action produce more momentum than another? These are the questions we'll ask and answer. (We will also use the physics definition for metaphorical purposes such as in the prior racing examples.)

Buses and Butterflies

Humans intuitively understand and respect physical momentum. We don't walk in front of moving buses; and not even the most reckless butterflies can make us fear for our lives.

Problem: *human momentum* isn't intuitive like physical momentum is. In a human life, those butterflies can morph into buses sometimes. Put in a pragmatic, terrifying way: just one butterfly-sized event, thought, or feeling can make or break a person's life if they preserve and compound that momentum.

People have let a single comment or instance of failure tear their life down. Others have turned one viral video into a lucrative career (Bhad Bhaby, Antoine Dodson, and the Ocean Spray skater come to mind). In each case, positive or negative, the small event becomes a source of leverage, and the rest is history.

Unfortunately, most people think of positive momentum in human lives as a "string of successes." That's not true momentum, though it may be the *result* of momentum. Consider sports, such as when a team goes on a scoring run. A winning streak is nice, but it only lasts as long as the force driving it persists.

Momentum in sports can change in an instant. With just one shot, one swing of the bat, one big play, a team can completely change the momentum of a game. What does this momentum mean if it can be so easily reversed in one play? It means that it isn't as concrete or strong as physics (or human) momentum. You won't see a bus going north at 60 MPH instantly change to go south at 60 MPH. It takes force, energy, and time to reverse its northern momentum and turn it into southern momentum.

Why do coaches take timeouts in basketball when the other team goes on a run? They want to reset their players' *mindsets* to a better place that will allow them to execute better. Timeouts also intend to break the other team's rhythm and momentum. And it often works! Or does it?

Many studies on basketball timeouts have small sample sizes and don't account for important variables, such as:

- You must possess the ball to call a timeout. Thus, the team calling the timeout always gets the ball first after the timeout. Scoring analysis after the timeout will naturally favor the team with first possession.
- With similar talent level, one should expect regression to the mean after one team goes on a

scoring run, regardless of timeouts taken.
- What if no timeout was called? Would the momentum have stayed the same or changed? A control is needed to know the value of timeout in terms of momentum.

For his senior thesis at Bryn Mawr, Sam Permutt studied the data from 3,690 basketball games and took these variables into account. He concluded (emphasis mine): "The data provides more support for the idea that the belief in momentum in sports **may be a perceptional bias** as opposed to an accurate depiction of the inner workings of a sport."[3]

Exactly right. The key phrase is "perceptional bias." Momentum in sports is a psychological, perception-based phenomenon. It can absolutely impact games. If one team gains confidence as the other loses it, the score will reflect that. This is not, however, the type of momentum we're after. It isn't strong enough.

This book isn't about some whimsical idea of "doing well recently." It's not even about the confidence shift you feel during a winning streak. Let's not forget that momentum in physics is a *real force*, and that's the type of momentum we need to guarantee success.

Real human momentum has force behind it; it doesn't rely on us thinking or feeling a certain way to bring

results.

As we get deeper into the book, you'll see more of this critical distinction between real and perceived momentum. When we remove these conversational ideas of human momentum, what remains is more concrete and far more powerful. Here's how I define real human momentum.

Human momentum accurately predicts how we'll behave in the future.

Nobody can guarantee future events, but they are highly predictable based on current momentum. Notice that sports momentum does not accurately predict future events. Consider that every huge comeback victory in sports history has required one thing—a massive deficit; this means the *other team* had significant momentum to begin the game and lost it in equally epic and rapid fashion. Human momentum is far more stable than that because it isn't based on perception.

Now that I've teased a key part of this book and highlighted a key breaking point from popular thought about momentum, I think we should address another important question.

How Much Does Momentum Matter in Our Lives?

Momentum matters more than you or I can fathom. Every person's primary aim should be to generate positive momentum in areas that matter to them. That's a bold statement, I know, but the reasoning in the next paragraph is bulletproof.

Positive momentum makes it easier to take positive actions. Taking positive actions then make it even easier to take additional positive actions. That's a compounding snowball of goodness. Meanwhile, negative momentum makes negative actions easier to take and can compound in *that* direction.

The secret to success is simple: Make it easier to succeed than to fail. Momentum doesn't merely do that, it does so exponentially.

Beyond the obvious and immediate result of our actions lies the total potential value of our actions. You can find the hidden value in actions by answering questions like:

- How might this action affect what I'll think, feel, and do next?
- Can this action change the trajectory of my day?
- Does this action have the potential to compound? If so, how much?

Positive momentum can bring your ideal lifestyle closer without additional effort. Negative momentum can make your ideal lifestyle nearly unobtainable. The momentum battle decides the war of where you want to go and who you want to be.

When Momentum Conquers Strength

In elementary school, we played "tug of war" during field day. In this game, two teams of about eight people tug on a rope, and whichever team can pull the rope to their side of the center line wins. This was the big event of field day. While the stronger teams usually won as expected, there were also some huge upsets.

How could a weaker team ever beat a stronger team in a game that's supposedly based on strength? Tug of war is mostly about strength, but not *only* about strength. It's also about momentum. Here are a couple tug-of-war momentum tricks to try if you're outmatched:

- **The jump:** Try to react faster to the starting whistle. If you pull hard enough before the other team matches you and sets their feet, you can run away with the win. Every team generally tries to start fast for this reason, but an overconfident, stronger team might let their guard down.
- **The rug pull:** If your team is facing stronger competition and they are winning, this is your last resort, but it's a good one. I've seen it work in real life and on the hit TV show *Squid Game*. With full tension on the rope and your team losing ground, your team will lunge *towards* the other team! If it works, the other team will fall backwards from the

unexpected loss of tension that had kept them upright. It will look as if somebody pulled a rug out from under their feet. Your team, still upright (and hopefully not across the center line yet), can then drag the other team across the finish line for the win before they regain their footing.

If you are losing in tug of war, your current state of momentum will lead to a loss. If the other team is stronger, your only chance is to change the momentum dynamic, even if that means giving the other team *more* momentum than they hoped for, as in the rug pull. And that is a very important lesson that we will revisit—more isn't always better!

Nobody Thinks about Their Momentum: Let's Change That

When's the last time you asked yourself, "Where's my momentum right now?" Never, I know. Yet that is often the correct and most powerful question you can ask yourself. Your answer will explain the way you feel about your life and the actions you (don't) take each day.

If you feel you lack positive momentum in your life, it's probably because you've never specifically tried to cultivate it. Instead, most people seek particular results or create specific goals to achieve. Momentum is a different beast and thus requires a different approach to action.

* * *

Casual conversations and sports have unfortunately defined the default idea of momentum in our lives, and that form of "momentum" is laughably weak compared to the real thing. What is the real thing, you ask? The four principles of human momentum will reveal everything you need to know.

Part One

The Four Principles of Human Momentum

The Magic of Momentum

We usually think of magic as something beyond explanation, something that defies natural laws and known principles. But some things are actually more magical *when* we understand them through observation and calculation.

Consider flight.

The physics of airplane flight are well documented, but you won't ever convince me that a 90,000-pound object soaring through the sky like a bird isn't magical. We didn't have access to this magic until relatively recently in human history. The Wright brothers' first successful plane flight happened in 1903.[1]

"It is possible to fly without motors, but not without knowledge and skill."
~ Wilbur Wright

Broadly, we can observe and explain human momentum—I will do my best to do so in this book—but its power will forever dazzle those who try to grasp it fully. The deeper we dig, and the more we master momentum's fundamental principles, the more magical momentum becomes to us, similar to marvelous technologies such as airplanes.

* * *

Let's be clear, though. The magic of flight can't compare to the magic of momentum. Human momentum has unfathomable power, which is why a hypervelocity star is a better comparison.

Wishing upon a Hypervelocity Star

HE 0437-5439 (or HVS3 for short) is a hypervelocity star cruising through space right now at 1.6 million miles per hour with a mass nearly nine times greater than the Sun.[2] HVS3 is bigger *and* faster than comprehension. This is a meta comparison, because this star's power actually lies in its preposterous momentum.

Scientists can compute HVS3's momentum with the numbers stated above, but what human can *comprehend* their real-world meaning? Excuse me, did you say 1.6 *million* MPH? Going just 100 MPH in a car feels fast. The fastest jet only goes 2,100 MPH, which is itself four times faster than the commercial airliners we're used to flying in. For anyone keeping track, we're talking about the fastest stuff we've got on Earth and we're not remotely close to 1.6 million MPH yet.

HVS3 is big, too. It is only nine times more massive than the sun, sure. But the sun is *333,000 times* more massive than our Earth. You could fit more than a million Earths inside the sun. Gadzooks!

Now try to imagine this behemoth star ripping through

space at 1.6 million MPH. It's literally unimaginable because we have no concept of anything this big or fast. We have the language, math, and tools to measure and communicate this star's attributes, yet it remains incomprehensible and more magical than Harry Potter. (I'm jk, JK.)

Like a hypervelocity star, momentum's magic is a product of its power—on a broad level, momentum is why the rich get richer, the strong get stronger, and the weak and poor get weaker and poorer. It's why some people soar into their wildest dreams and others fall into an endless abyss of misery. It continually rewards those who solve its mysteries and respect its might with compounding upward success. Those who believe themselves invincible, passively ignore its force, or otherwise don't understand how momentum works can fall to shocking depths of despair.

Our journey begins with four plainly worded principles because they reveal the *mechanisms* of momentum; they will increase our understanding of it. When you know a mechanism, you can use it and (later) master it.

Give Momentum a Blank Slate

To build a plane that can fly, the Wright brothers had to learn about the mechanics of flight, engines, physics, propellers, aerodynamics, take-off, landing, and so on. But before all of that could happen, they needed to redefine their idea of what *can* fly.

The Wright brothers had to separate the principles of flight from their prior observational understanding of flight. Their plane weighed over 600 pounds, which was unlike anything that had flown before. At that time, everything else we knew that flew was lightweight (and alive with *flapping* wings!).[3] I'll be honest—if it were me, I'd have laughed off the idea of a 600-pound machine flying (as many did).

It isn't intuitive to think that a heavy object can fly. But this is what makes principles so valuable—they can reveal all truths, including those that aren't intuitive. Someone who understands the principles of aerodynamics can understand why planes, helicopters, ~~superman,~~ *and* butterflies can all fly.

To discover the magic of momentum, then, we must strip away our prior "conversational understanding" of it. As with the Wright brothers, we will unlock new possibilities by looking at the principles of momentum and finding those less intuitive truths. As you read further, I encourage you to redefine what you think momentum is and what it means in your life. I'm going to show you how to fly… figuratively speaking.

Principle 1

You Are Most Likely to Do What You Just Did (Short-Term Momentum)

You are most likely to do what you just did.

This is where we begin. This humble sentence is the heart of momentum.

For such a simple, obvious idea, it carries life-changing power. I've already changed my life thanks to this principle, so I have no qualms making that claim. This is closer to a known quantity of physics than a hunch.

Isaac Newton's first law of motion states that an object at rest or in motion will not change its state unless acted upon by an external force.[1] Newton's law is about physics, of course, but it works very well as a personal development metaphor.[2]

Why Momentum instead of Motion?

With the mention of Newton's first law of *motion*, you might wonder why this book talks about momentum instead of motion. What's the difference, anyway?

Motion creates momentum, and that momentum influences subsequent motion.

You could say that momentum measures the "oomph" of motion in a particular direction; it concerns the power, direction, and potential of motion (in physics and in human lives).

Momentum vs Motion Example: Pollen drifting in the wind and a fired bullet are both in motion, but a fired bullet carries significantly more momentum.

There is no momentum without motion. But momentum is the prize. We will work backwards from the prize to determine optimal strategies to turn our motion into momentum.

We are always in motion. In human behavior, even inaction can be considered "behavioral motion." It's the **momentum** of that motion that makes it so meaningful. Running in circles is motion that takes you nowhere (known as angular momentum in physics). Running to the bathroom is motion with speed, meaning, and purpose (linear momentum)!

Everyone already understands that doing something positive is better than doing nothing. Not everyone understands the need to optimize their approach to action for momentum instead of results. A result is a one-time payment; momentum can pay you for life.

Be careful not to jump to conclusions or oversimplify at this point, as more momentum, even in the right direction, is not always better. A speeding car may get to its destination faster, but the risk outweighs the reward. That's why we have speed limits. And be sure to remember the bullet and pollen example of momentum. We will revisit that later... with a plot twist!

Why We Sit through Bad Movies

Now let's get into what this principle means for your life. You are most likely to do what you just did. So what? Well, have you ever finished a movie you didn't enjoy? If a movie is bad, but not too painful to watch, most people will still finish it. Isn't that remarkable?

Have you ever seen the movie *Copper Mountain?* I watched it. Not half of it. All of it. I kept waiting and hoping for it to get good because it stars Jim Carrey. I love Jim Carrey, but this movie is possibly the worst I've ever seen. (And yes, I've seen *The Room*. Great film. Hi, Mark!)

* * *

Terrible movies are not the direst consequence of negative momentum. People die from drug and alcohol overdoses, too. Drugs are so dangerous in part because our primary resistance to them comes from the very area of the brain that they impair (prefrontal cortex).

You're most likely to do what you just did, even if it's watching an awful movie or taking harmful substances.

This is the first principle of momentum because it's fundamental. Every action you take creates momentum in that same direction.

So far, I've only given examples of negative momentum. Do you know why? I'm not being negative for the fun of it. Rather, these examples reveal its raw power. Preexisting desire obfuscates most positive momentum examples—*we already want to do these things*, so it is difficult to see that power at work.

Of course we will finish watching a great movie, eating a delicious home-cooked meal, or doing the dishes once we've started. All of those things benefit us more than they hurt us, giving us an incentive to continue. It's the *net negative* things we continue to do in the short term that show how impactful momentum can be.

If given a choice between great and terrible, we will always choose great… unless we've already started with terrible, in which case we may stay with terrible simply because we're already moving in that direction.

The Crux of Human Momentum's First Principle

There's a way to think about the first principle that will help you when you need to decide what to do in the moment. To explain it, we need to cover the physics definition of momentum (briefly). I promise there's no homework!

Momentum in physics measures how difficult something is to stop or slow down.

Momentum = mass x velocity (velocity = direction + speed)

That's physics. But let's convert it into human momentum. For that, I like to change mass into power. The mass of a moving bus is like the *power* of a habit (both are hard to stop once they get going). Habitual behaviors also carry "weight" in your mind and natural preferences.

Habits are neural pathways in the brain that act like "rails." When the brain encounters a situation for which it has already developed a habitual response, the associated neural pathway fires. After that, it's usually autopilot. With strategy or effort, you may divert from the rails (the habit); otherwise, you're going on that predictable path. Habits are the known powerhouse of human behavior.

If you accept the change of mass to power, that gives us three major factors of *human momentum*: power, direction, and speed. One of these far outweighs the others in importance, but I bet you can't guess it.

For *human momentum*, which of these do you think is most important for generating and sustaining positive momentum? What matters most? Take a moment to think about it.

- A. The **power** of our actions
- B. The **direction** of our actions
- C. The **speed** of our actions

Have an answer? If not, take a guess. This will be interesting, regardless of what you choose.

...

...

...

The Correct Answer is...
B. Direction! Most of you probably picked power. To be

fair, I've written four books on habits, habits represent power, and I just wrote about it a few paragraphs ago. But for human momentum, there is a clear order of importance and **direction** wins outright. The order pertains to sequential focus. Direction must always come first!

1. Direction
2. Power
3. Speed

There are two reasons that direction is most important.

First, even weak and slow momentum in the right direction is of <u>significant</u> benefit. (Insert tortoise vs hare parable here.) Consider this: Power and speed are *only* beneficial if applied in the right direction. Their utility is 100% dependent on that factor. This is true in the physical world and in human lives. In the wrong direction, I think we can agree that power and speed are quite detrimental!

"You're most likely to do what you just did" is purely a statement of direction. If you're headed west, you'll most likely go where next? West, of course. I didn't mention your power or speed of travel, and yet, we still know the answer is west because this first principle is true.

You're most likely to go west if your most recent step was in that direction.

* * *

The second reason direction matters most? The all-important power of habits to form a behavioral foundation for our lives *begins with the ability to choose the same direction frequently (usually every day)*. In time, the habit (power) comes. So once again, even for something as important and powerful as our habits, we need direction *first*.

Golden nugget: Always concern yourself with your direction first; once in motion, you can think about power and speed.

Change Your Direction, Change Your Life

The most life-changing moment of my life began with a momentary change of direction. On December 29th, 2012, after failing to get motivated to exercise, I did one push-up, mostly as a joke. That single push-up, however unimpressive, changed my direction from sedentary to exercising, and I'm a different person today because of it.

After my one push-up, I gradually built more momentum until I had completed a 30-minute workout. On a day that I had zero motivation and no willpower to force a workout, momentum (that this first principle speaks of) single-handedly carried me to a substantial result that seemed impossible. After that experience, I committed to do one push-up (or more) every day and wrote about the strategy in my book *Mini Habits* a year later.

Just as this principle suggests, whenever I did a single

push-up, I often did more of them (or other exercises). Critically, not once was it habit that turned my one push-up into more exercise; it was short-term momentum. Always momentum. Every time you embark on a new direction, you create instant short-term momentum. Do not underestimate what that momentum can do.

What Does it Mean to Pursue Direction First?

One push-up a day is what I call a mini habit, which is a *commitment to a particular direction every day*. Most arbitrary, preset goals actively neglect direction because they only accept the direction of a particular quality or quantity (all or nothing).

People will say things like, "I will work out for an hour every day." That *intends* direction—all goals do—but what happens when they don't hit their lofty target reveals their true priority. They don't work out for 39 minutes. They don't do 23 minutes. *They do nothing at all.* **Instead of creating a small amount of momentum in a positive direction, they accept negative momentum and continue in aimlessness or, worse, bad habits.**

You might think, "Hold up, these aren't mutually exclusive. Why can't you go in the right direction with more than one weak-sauce push-up?"

This question implies a false dichotomy, that doing one push-up is at odds with your desire to... do push-ups!

***

Does doing one push-up make it more or less likely that you will do additional push-ups or other exercise? Any number of push-ups, even one, makes it *far more likely* that you'll do *extra* push-ups. And that flips the question on its head.

It's actually because direction and power/speed are not mutually exclusive (i.e., you can attain them together) that focusing on direction first is always correct. A direction-first mindset never prevents you from generating power and speed; it always helps!

The world loves overly ambitious goals, but it's difficult, if not completely irrational, to argue against the prioritization of direction. Would you ever slam on the gas with your car pointed directly at a llama? (If you would, why do you hate llamas so much?) Get your direction correct first before you even *think* about power and speed. Otherwise, you'll wreck your car and ruin a beautiful llama's day.

This first principle is about prioritizing direction to gain momentum in the short term. Our most recent action is most likely our next action, and the chain reaction doesn't end there! Next, we're going to talk about long-term momentum, and that happens deep in the brain's subconscious.

Principle 2

Consistent Action over Time Kills Resistance (Long-Term Momentum)

In a very general way, the brain is a two-part system, one designed for energy efficiency and the other for power.[1]

Brain Part 1, the energy-efficient autopilot: The subconscious (basal ganglia) gives us energy-efficient "autopilot actions." These are habits—do this thing and get a reward. "Reward" can mean anything from a clean mouth (brushing your teeth) to taste and satisfaction (eating chocolate) to pain relief (taking medicine). These autopilot actions require little to no thought and thus use almost no mental energy from deliberation.

Brain Part 2, the powerful manual pilot: The conscious part of our brain (prefrontal cortex) gives us power to override autopilot actions when we have the will and energy to do so. It enables us to shape our behavior and our lives with deliberate planning and action. But there's a limit to how much we can control, seeing as we don't have unlimited time, energy, or willpower to live perfect lives. The best advice in the world can't save us from suboptimal living.

It's important to understand the limits of these two behavior systems. When you do, you can utilize *both* of them better.

- **The basal ganglia, a group of "subcortical nuclei" in your brain, can't rationalize away bad habits or convince themselves to eat more spinach.** In the long term, they value proven processes over planning, and, in the short term, they value rewards over rationality. That's why they need help from the prefrontal cortex, which sees the entire consequential picture of actions we take.
- **The prefrontal cortex can veto or force an alternative action because it knows better, but only when it cares to AND has the energy for it.** Like most powerful things, it requires a lot of energy to operate. Thus, it tires us out and/or doesn't work when we're tired from something else. Studies show that, when stressed or overwhelmed, we rely on our habits (good and bad). That's autopilot stepping in for an exhausted pilot.

* * *

Beneath consciousness, we have thoughts and emotions that we don't (directly) choose. And it's tricky, because these "rogue" thoughts and emotions mix in seamlessly with our consciousness. It's difficult to tell them apart. Are these arguments valid or are they subconscious justifications for doing something I feel like doing but know I shouldn't do?

We use our autopilot system (a lot) in life. Autopilot follows predetermined procedures and protocols, meaning it's *predictable*. Bingo. Anything that generates predictable future behavior is real human momentum.

Long-term momentum is that inner nudge to do certain things, at certain times, and in a certain way. It often manifests as self-persuasion. You may think of habits as automated mindless processes, but they are also active lobbyists in your head, persuading you with various thoughts and emotions to do their favorite behaviors again and again. Just as big corporations spend millions on lobbyists to get favorable outcomes for their company (corrupt as they may be), habits lobby our brains to continue doing favored behaviors (for better and worse).

The next time you shower, pay attention to how you dry off. I'd bet that you do it the same way every time. Your drying-off pattern is a habit that accurately predicts your behavior after showers you haven't taken yet. That's long-term momentum! Unless you consciously choose to change that dry-off pattern, it will remain. We don't change it because it would take more effort and who cares if you dry your knees first every time? Yeah, that's the weirdest body part to start with and I'm judging you for it, but dry is dry, and any towel pattern that dries you is fine.

A towel-drying routine is a nonsignificant example of significant long-term momentum. But how does long-term momentum—in towel drying or something else—form in the first place?

The Unfair Battle between Broccoli and Heroin

What percentage of addicts planned their addiction *before the first dose*? How many people have said, "Today is the day I begin a heroin addiction"? Zero people, I imagine. And although nobody chooses this path deliberately, it happens a lot.[2]

Most addictive substances require little effort to take, and the brain-altering reward is immediate and substantial. Taking even one dose of any addictive drug is a risk. It's actually disrespectful (to your subconscious) and naïve to try an addictive substance and assume you can stop. Even a doctor-prescribed opioid must be taken with extreme caution.

From the National Institute of Drug Abuse: "Between 8 and 12 percent of people using an opioid for chronic pain develop an opioid use disorder. An estimated 4 to 6 percent who misuse prescription opioids transition to heroin."

People lose this battle all the time. With their lives literally on the line, people often cannot curb serious addictions. There are many famous cases of it. These people were not weak. Long-term momentum is *that* strong (especially when combined with brain-altering substances).

Ahem. On a more cheerful note, how many broccoli addicts exist? Five? I don't know. Not many. I quite like (cooked) broccoli, but broccoli *addiction* is not possible for me because the immediate reward isn't strong enough.[3] Broccoli has its merits, but you have to get to know them.

Behavior Reward Structures and the Brain

The worst things for us feel (very) good now but hurt us later, whether it's food, drugs, or miscellaneous irresponsibilities. The best things for us often feel neutral or even bad now and much better later, such as broccoli, honesty, saving money, and deadlifts. Bottom line: healthy behaviors are harder to learn because the reward structure is not as obvious, enticing, and upfront as something like a sugar or drug high.

With a strong preference for immediate rewards, the basal ganglia appear to be designed to make us kill ourselves with pleasure as we avoid "boring" things like broccoli. If so, why are most people able to avoid hard drugs and even eat their greens sometimes?[4] Assuming you are operating under your own free will and your mom doesn't control your food intake, it's possible to choose broccoli over cocaine because the prefrontal cortex steps in.

People know drugs are dangerous and broccoli is healthy. Consciously, most people prefer healthy broccoli over dangerous cocaine. Subconsciously, however, if given a taste of each, the brain will prefer cocaine to broccoli.

To be clear, our fight isn't against our own subconscious (basal ganglia). Not initially, anyway. While they sound villainous, the basal ganglia are actually *neutral*. Humans are just masters of destruction. If you pour soda on your laptop and the laptop malfunctions, don't blame the laptop. If you take cocaine, don't blame the brain for malfunctioning. That's what drugs do to brains!

Bad habits are easy-to-access, tempting rewards, and that's why we all seem to end up with some of them. An autopilot system that prefers the path of least resistance and easiest rewards can lead us to scary addictions and low broccoli consumption. But that's not the end of the story. Let's shift to how we can fine-tune this autopilot system for our benefit.

Your subconscious can be a powerful force for good if managed with knowledge-driven intention. Even if the basal ganglia resist a healthy behavior initially, that doesn't mean it's game over. Luckily for us, there's a secret weapon that this part of the brain prefers even more than rewards. Yes, *even more than rewards*.

The Power of Familiarity

Bad habits are easy to form *initially* because they lure us in with easy rewards. The allure of an easy reward gets us to try something. Then, repeated exposure gets us hooked. Repeated exposure creates significant familiarity with the entire process—the cue, the behavior, and the juicy reward.

The subconscious brain loves nothing more than familiarity.

Do you want to know just how much the brain values familiarity? Daniel Kahneman says in *Thinking, Fast and Slow*, "A reliable way to make people believe in falsehoods is frequent repetition, because familiarity is not easily distinguished from truth."

To the brain, familiarity is on the same level as truth. Truth is everything to us. Any religious beliefs and values we have are based on what we believe is true about the world. Our beliefs are so important to us that we choose them over just about everything else, even our own lives.

As I type this, Russia is invading Ukraine. The USA offered

to give Ukrainian President Volodymyr Zelensky—a primary target of Russia's massive and dangerous military—a safe passage out of the war zone into safety. His response?

"The fight is here; I need ammunition, not a ride."

This man is worth millions of dollars, in a position of power, with every excuse to protect himself and ensure his own safety. Instead, he chose to stay and fight with his people. Why? He believes it's right. He believes that Ukraine is a sovereign nation and is willing to risk his life for it. I don't know what will ultimately happen in this war, but Zelensky's decision is an honorable, powerful response to what he believes is true.

Familiarity is on *that level*; on the level of your deepest values; on the level of your greatest convictions; familiarity is so strong because the subconscious has no defense against it.

The subconscious is so highly moldable via repetition and familiarity that it's possible to believe things we would otherwise know as false!

The quote by Kahneman, if you believe it, or if I repeat it enough times (wink), suggests that humans value and trust familiarity as much or more than the truth itself. Many people would deny this. But it happens sneakily, beneath our consciousness. The more familiar something is, the deeper it sinks into your subconscious, safer and safer from the pointed questions of your consciousness.

The Deception of the Familiar

If we love familiarity, why do people enjoy unusual experiences like shark cages and skydiving? Well, there is a collective human familiarity there, even though most individuals haven't done them. In addition, people find other desires to compete with familiarity. There's significant notoriety, excitement, pleasure, and even fame associated with being a pioneer or trying something novel.

Millions of people skydive every year. But how many people would volunteer to try it first? The first successful parachute jump was in 1797. That was a brave guy.[5]

The risk of skydiving highlights a great example of how I personally cannot distinguish familiarity from truth. In the US, there are about 20 skydiving deaths out of 3.3 million jumps annually. Seeing that data, with my luck, I would seriously hesitate to skydive. And yet, I *casually* take a far greater risk every day.

I've never been skydiving, but I've driven a car countless times over the last 20 years. Yet skydiving is statistically much less dangerous than driving a car.[6] One wrong move in the car at 75 MPH is likely instant death. In addition, even if I drive perfectly, something beyond my control—

say, a drunk driver— can still kill me.

Despite all that, you know, *factual stuff*, I know driving. I don't know skydiving like I know driving. And apparently, that's enough to override hard data. Even having researched it, written about it, and admitted the truth of it just now, even understanding the familiarity bias, I confess I'd *still* feel safer driving than skydiving. Either I'm crazy or familiarity is unbelievably powerful (Ha! False dichotomy again! Both are true.). That's typical of familiarity—you can throw hard facts at it and it still won't budge!

Familiarity alone makes car driving seem safer than a great number of things that are actually safer than getting behind the wheel. When you're going 80 MPH on the highway, are you constantly thinking about how you're in a dangerous, speeding death machine that kills people every day? I mean, that's the truth. We tell ourselves stories that may not be true because of familiarity.

I don't mean to suggest that everything we believe is a lie, only that familiarity is more influential to us on a deep, almost untouchable level than nearly anything else; it distorts everyone's perception of truth and reality.

Unless familiar behaviors are 100% loathsome, they are the ultimate brain reward. Why else would people stay in unpleasant situations and continue harmful patterns? They prefer a familiar, bad life over an unknown (possibly worse, probably better) life.

People stay in unfulfilling, unhealthy relationships regularly. It's as common as dirt. These situations may be bad, but they are *known*, which can outweigh the pain that would otherwise drive the desire for change.

Earlier, we talked about finishing bad movies and drug overdoses as examples of short-term momentum. Just as with short-term momentum, the negative examples of familiarity (chronic lying, bad relationships, driving cars nonchalantly, etc.) are the most eye-opening examples of its power for long-term momentum. Familiarity can compel us to make bad, painful choices for *years*. Brushing aside how sad that is, how *incredible* is that?

If you can't understand why you or someone you love is destroying their life, consider all that we've covered here. It's likely they are doing their best but are caught in a negative momentum storm that they don't know how to (or are too scared to attempt to) escape from. I promise I'm not writing this book to make you sad. I needed to use those examples to show you that momentum is more powerful than Thanos with every infinity stone.

This will sound strange, but I have to say it. We give too much blame and praise to people for the state of their lives. We all do our best as a general rule, right? But what if we do our best with a terrible strategy that gives us no chance to succeed? What if we do our best in a toxic environment without the knowledge we need to escape or the wherewithal to do it? In both cases, we're in trouble, and not for a lack of trying.

Everyone sees the luck involved in a person who inherits wealth rather than earning it, but what about people born into other types of exceptional situations? Malcolm Gladwell talks about this in his book *Outliers*, noticing that a disproportionate number of hockey players are born in January–March, or that a lot of software tycoons were born around 1955. And these are just the obvious, big examples. Instead of a golden spoon, some people are born with a golden platter containing various golden utensils of positive environmental momentum.

People are eager to make judgments about themselves and others without considering less personal, more impactful factors first. If you don't understand the power of momentum and how to manage it and you make a couple of poor choices, it can send your whole life off the rails, causing you to make even worse choices. Even too much positive momentum—as in the case of many lottery winners—can destroy your life if you don't know how to handle it (picture the tug-of-war team getting the rug pulled out from under them).

Others don't see the initial choices or circumstances that

created the momentum that leads to the worst choices. They see those awful choices as the beginning of the story. "He robbed a bank. She cheated on her exam. He drove drunk." None of those things happen randomly. They are the unfortunate culmination of a series of choices that compounded chaotically in the wrong direction. It's not fair, but, as I said to begin this book, *momentum is never fair*. It can lift you up or crush you beyond what is reasonable. Respect it.

Familiarity Can Create a Better Life Too

Back into lighthearted mode? Wheeeee! I'm most interested in sharing solutions, and familiarity leads us to a very good one.

Consider this: If you wanted, you could easily train yourself to slap the wall every time you went into the bathroom. In fact, I bet that there is at least one person who already does this. Isn't that interesting in a stupid way? This action gives no real benefit to the person doing it, and it's pointless, but if they've done it for long enough, they'll *prefer* to do it in the future just because it is the most familiar way to enter the bathroom.

People have many idiosyncrasies that they repeat for no other reason than familiarity and habit. Does anyone else avoid stepping on cracks on the sidewalk? I blame the person in elementary school who once told me, "Step on a crack and you'll break your mother's back." I, a fully grown man with grey hair in my beard, still avoid sidewalk cracks sometimes for my mom. I'm not superstitious, I'm familiar.

To visualize the power of an action to create long-term momentum, picture someone slapping that wall every day or avoiding cracks on the sidewalk. If you can train wall slapping and crack dodging (double meaning!), you can train yourself to prefer nearly any behavior. The example of people repeating painful patterns may be a more compelling proof of our defenselessness against familiarity, but it's also depressing, so let's stick with the classic wall slap. Huzzah!

Familiarity (which can later become habit) is the essential long-term momentum factor of an action. When you take an action even one time, you gain a small amount of familiarity with it, the trigger that prompted it, and whatever reward (if any) you associate with it. That exposure is critical to the brain's long-term preferences, *even if you found the experience somewhat bland or unrewarding.*

I find it important to distinguish between familiarity and habit here because familiarity happens before habit. Before we even take an action for the first time, familiarity through external sources (videos, instructional training, stories, etc.) can increase our comfort level and willingness to try.

* * *

People think they need to pair habits with external rewards for them to stick. That's not necessarily true. Rewards can help reinforce behaviors, yes, but familiarity alone can drive habit formation because the brain sees familiarity as appealing or as a reward in itself.

I'm not saying that habits aren't powerful. I'd have to delete my other books if I did! Habits are the mature, late-stage form of familiarity. That power *begins* with familiarity, and that's why I think it's important to highlight it. When you want to change your behavior, you must do whatever you can to establish familiarity and regularity with this new way of living.

Now, the negative examples in these first two principles of momentum show their power to wreck us, but we can create powerful positive momentum just the same. The next principle exposes a "fake" kind of momentum, something that many people unfortunately see as real momentum.

Principle 3

Perceived Momentum Is Not Real Momentum (The Myth of Speed)

Remember when we discussed the components of human momentum?

1. Direction (near-term momentum)
2. Power (long-term momentum)
3. Speed (???)

We've identified the first two as near-term and long-term momentum, respectively. As for speed... well, I only listed it out of courtesy to the original physics metaphor. This next sentence may drop your jaw. Ready?

Behavioral speed kills human momentum!

I understand that it's an odd claim and seemingly defies

the laws of physics. But I'm talking specifically about *human* momentum. Our momentum is unique. Sorry, not every physics metaphor is going to translate one-to-one to complex concepts. The metaphor still provides useful ideas, just not the ideas one would expect.

Speed is a variable measurement. When I say speed isn't a part of human momentum, I mean that the pursuit of high speed deters human momentum because of what it sacrifices.

Speedy Thinking

Speed measures distance covered in a period of time. For example, cars can drive 60 miles (distance covered) per hour (time). People most often think of their goals in terms of speed. They want to reach a certain destination (distance covered) in a set period of time. Examples might include:

- Work out 30 minutes every day for 30 days (900 minutes of exercise progress in 30 days)
- Meditate 30 minutes a day for 30 days (900 minutes of meditation in 30 days)
- Clean eating for 30 days (90 clean meals consumed in 30 days)
- Practice violin 30 minutes a day for 30 days (900 minutes of violin in 30 days)
- Smoothie or juice "cleanse" for 10 days (30 smoothies consumed in 10 days)
- NaNoWriMo: Write 50,000 words in a month

- Read five books by October
- Lose 30 pounds this year

Each of these goals is based on speed, as they give a specific time to achieve a specific result, which provides a milestone and/or an expected benefit. Speed-based goals can work, but their structure deters momentum. Before we get into why that happens, let's discuss their benefits first.

The Benefit of Speed-Based Goals

This is not a hit job on traditional goal-setting. I want to be fair and kind, so I will explain the positive aspects of these goals before destroying them.

The primary and unquestioned benefit of a speed-based goal is **intent**. If you can clarify your intent into specific actions, you are far more likely to take action. The upside of 30-day challenges is that they set clear intentions for each of the days. That's good.

Clear intention is the prerequisite for any non-habitual action. Without intention, you're living on autopilot.

The other benefits of such a goal are the satisfaction and results you get when you complete it. You set a(n arbitrary) milestone, and reach it, and feel good about it. That can motivate you to see to the end and get your reward.

Last, 30-day challenges are ideal for experimentation. If

you want to try something to see if you like it, such as cold showers, do it for a week to a month. That's fine.

This book, however, isn't for experiments, it's for changing or even transforming your life with momentum. There are certain things in life that you *know* you want to improve, that you *know* will benefit you if you do them consistently. Exercise is the most common one, but there's also healthy eating, work productivity, house upkeep/cleaning, financial planning, communication skills, organization, and meditation. It's in the most critical areas of life where real momentum shines and speed-based goals don't work well.

The Core Problem with Speed-Based Goals

Speed-based goals are also time-based goals, as time is part of how we measure speed. Time is useful for many reasons, but speed-based goals take place over a multi-day time period; that is the very worst time period to use.

Any time-based goal that exceeds the one-day time period is inherently flawed and lacks real momentum.

Do you know why? It's human biology. It's sleep.

Everyone I know sleeps. If you don't sleep (or abide by a polyphasic sleep schedule or are a vampire), the following doesn't apply to you—you four vamps can skip this section. But if you sleep, this is important!

* * *

After living a day, humans sleep about eight hours to recharge. This is the structure of human life. Maybe you sleep more or less, but sleep is always the buffer between our days.

The body and brain slow down *drastically* during sleep to recover from stress (mental, physical, cellular, etc.). So let me ask you... After lying unconscious and your body shutting down, barely moving for eight(ish) hours, how do you maintain the momentum you had from the previous day?

You don't. You lose all of it. That's okay, but you have to live accordingly.

Between the physiological changes in sleep, the time passed, and the conscious–unconscious–conscious pattern, you don't have any momentum when you wake up. It's like a computer restart, in which everything returns to its original state.

Remember the first principle of momentum? *You are most likely to do what you just did.* That is **always** where your short-term momentum lies. You can't be sewing a shirt and also have some short-term momentum in rugby, unless you're doing both at the same time. That sounds like a dangerous, albeit exciting, sport I would love to watch. If you're sewing, you're (probably) not playing rugby. Thus, if you're sleeping or waking up from sleeping, you have **zero** short-term momentum from your previous day's endeavors. ZERO!

When you wake up in the morning, your momentum is not technically neutral, as people who feel groggy or glued to their beds in the morning can attest. You could say that *the new day* is neutral, but every moment in your life carries momentum according to the first principle, including sleep. I don't know about you, but I've had many naps extend beyond my plans. I've pressed snooze. That's sleepy momentum at work.

Good Morning: Your State of Momentum Is...

Resting in bed is your state of momentum upon waking up. It's recommended to use the energy you gained from sleep to get up and get your day started. Mornings are your first opportunity to create positive momentum for the day!

Many people are (rightly) obsessed with morning routines and healthy sleep practices because each sets you up with an easier positive momentum ramp to start the day. In addition, in the morning—once your hormones adjust or you cheat with caffeine—you should be at or near peak energy for the day. And, needless to say, the earlier in the day you create positive momentum, the more time it has to benefit you.

What does all of this say about a 10-day goal? It means that

10-day goals carry no short-term momentum. If you must do something for only 10 days and still want to benefit from momentum, you must think of it as 10 one-day goals, since there is no momentum carryover from day to day.

Create new short-term momentum every day or you will get off track at some point.

I'm telling you that success on day one does nothing for day two. But... doesn't it? Anecdotally, I know I feel better about day two if I succeeded on day one. That's result-driven confidence or, as I call it, perceived momentum. I also call it "fake" momentum, because it doesn't work like the other two we've covered.

Perceived (Fake) Momentum

Human momentum is not a single thing that we have and use throughout all periods of time; it's a force that operates by **two specific mechanisms** in two different time periods, near-term and long-term.

Near-term and long-term momentum guide us to do more of the same thing, but how they accomplish that feat is not the same.

Intraday momentum is driven by what we might call "behavioral physics." Long-term momentum is driven by neurological changes in the brain after months or years of doing something.[1]

There is a large, ridiculous, awkward gap between those time periods. Beyond the single day, we have to wait for months or *years* for momentum reinforcements? Yes. But, perhaps because of its awkwardness, we assume that gap isn't there. I think it's a bit like peripheral vision, in which the brain "fills in" visual gaps.

Our eyes can only focus on a tiny area, but our brains do a lot of creative work to map out the rest, making our vision seem more like a full picture. Designed illusions have shown that the brain can make us see what isn't actually there. They say that seeing is believing, but in some cases, believing becomes seeing (what isn't there).

Because we have two specific mechanisms of momentum that we can see and understand (near- and long-term), it seems reasonable to assume there's no momentum dead spot between them, but there sure is. We believe it should be there, and voila, we think we see it, too.

The Placebo Effect: Momentum Edition

Perceived momentum is a placebo effect. Like any placebo effect, it absolutely does work sometimes. It is relevant. But it remains a fabrication of the mind. We can't rely upon it in the same way we can rely on real momentum.

* * *

You could put it as financial managers do: "past performance does not necessarily predict future results." People read that, and then ignore it. They say, "But this fund has returned 20% for four years in a row!" Then Bernie Madoff and 2008 happen. I digress.

To be clear, two weeks of success *feels like* momentum. It mimics real momentum convincingly. The difference is that real momentum doesn't disappear without a fight, whereas perceived momentum can and does.

When you do something for 30 days, you've established some familiarity with the behavior and will have made some progress in developing long-term momentum. *It's just not the type of progress people think it is.* Habits at this stage are very, very weak and will easily be usurped by your other habits if you aren't careful.[2] It is meaningful progress, but you're closer to day one than you are to being done in terms of momentum.

Doing something for 30 days won't usually carry the game-changing momentum people think it will, let alone just a week or two. Why give yourself only 30 days to win a war that takes years to win? I get that it's less intimidating to aim for 30 days, but that's a case of the right idea and the wrong application.

When you do something daily for a number of days in a row, it's a good result that will increase your confidence.

That's meaningful, absolutely, but it isn't as resilient as momentum. It's so tricky to explain this because most people see momentum as a string of successes instead of the mechanism that brings you success. But I think the following section will clarify what I mean.

Confidence from Results vs Confidence from Processes

Time-based goals, speed-based goals, and mid-term momentum all represent the same thing—seeking a particular result in an amount of time. Importantly, even though this strategy is flawed, it can still produce short- and long-term momentum. For example, if you aim to work out for an hour every day for a year, every day that you actually start to work out generates short-term momentum that will help you finish your workout and make your day better. And doing it several days creates a small amount of long-term momentum.

The problem, and the reason this method kills momentum, is that it focuses on *results*. That makes it unreliable, risky, and prone to sudden failure. You do the behavior to reach an arbitrary milestone (result). You only consider it a success if you get that result. You're probably motivated to do it for a specific benefit (a result). Everything relies on the result, whether it's meeting your behavioral objective for the day or getting a benefit because of meeting the objective.

* * *

Results are finicky.

If you set out to do 100 push-ups a day, that's mostly in your control, but there are constant internal (motivation, fatigue) and external factors (injury, busyness) that can derail it. Even worse, if you're able to stick with your pursuit, the hopeful result of getting in shape may take longer than expected. This uncertainty and challenge is *for an action that you have almost total control over*. Imagine goals in which you have to rely on the actions and judgment of others! Yikes!

Most goals people set are result-driven. That's a problem.

Result-driven goals get in their own way. For example, if you were to modify a human brain for shooting a basketball, the first thing you would do is remove the part of the brain that cares about the result of each shot. Do you know why? Because the result of your previous shot has nothing to do with making or missing the next shot, or at least it shouldn't. It isn't involved in the process, and so can only hurt. In real human brains, makes and misses can affect our confidence level, which affects our next shot too! Do you see where I'm going with this? ~~Brain surgery!~~

A basketball shot is determined by two things—muscle memory and execution. Muscle memory involves the mechanical movement(s) required for a successful shot. Michael Jordan famously attempted a free throw shot in a game with his eyes closed. He'd taken so many thousand free throws that he remembered the precise mechanics required for a successful free throw. And, yes, he made it.

But even the best shooters with finely tuned muscle memory miss shots. Why? The human element interferes with the *execution* of known mechanics.

Hot Shooter, Cold Shooter

Like momentum over a 10-day period, the idea of a basketball player getting hot or cold is completely valid, *but only as a placebo effect*. Players get hot because they think they are; they make more shots than usual because their confidence rises. Confidence improves execution because, as it increases, a player **worries less** and is **less distractable** when shooting.

When a player is missing shots, however, what does that do? It depends on the player's mental discipline. If they have that custom-designed brain with result-caring taken out, it will have zero effect. But if the player relies upon excellent results to play confidently (or is human), missed shots may cause overthinking, worrying, and hesitance to shoot, all of which will negatively impact shooting performance. That's why cold shooting can easily lead to more cold shooting.

Elite players try not to let misses affect their confidence or next shot. The late basketball legend Kobe Bryant was once asked about Deron Williams shooting 0-for-9 in a game. He replied, "I would go 0-for-30 before I would go 0-for-9. 0-for-9 means you beat yourself, you psyched yourself out of the game, because Deron Williams can get more shots in the game. The only reason is because you've just now lost confidence in yourself."[3]

Kobe Bryant was famous for having unshakeable confidence. He did not base his confidence on whether he made or missed shots: his confidence was in himself, his preparation, and his skills. There's a lot we can learn from that sentiment.

Short-term and long-term momentum are like the mechanics of a basketball shot. If you place your confidence in those, you will *naturally* generate positive results and confidence. They are the key to success!

The Folly of Riding the Results Wave

When you base your confidence on recent results, your confidence will crater as soon as your results do, *which will create even worse results*. That second part is the killer. That means you've given up on creating positive momentum (even though you can create it instantly) just because your perceived confidence dropped momentarily. Are your failed goals now flashing before your eyes? This is why they failed. You were fine, but you fell into the trap.

Dr. Donald Wetmore says, "90% of those who join health

and fitness clubs will stop going within the first 90 days." This is, not coincidentally, smack dab in the mid-term time frame. Within 90 days is not the first day, and it's not after a year or two.

Those who rely on the façade of mid-term momentum will behave exactly like Deron Williams did in Kobe's quote. They'll behave just like Dr. Wetmore's statistic suggests. Everyone reading this book knows it, because it has happened to all of us.

If missing a shot harms your confidence, you will fail sooner than later, because nobody is "always on." Nobody shoots 100%. Those who pursue mid-term (perceived) momentum struggle when they face resistance to their plans.

How to Win 99.9952% of the Time

Real momentum is special because it carries a near-100% success rate. It's a mathematical probability. Perceived momentum, though, is all over the place. It can produce demoralizing failure as easily as incredible success.

You don't have to "take my word" for these numbers. Decide yourself how reliable these are. But let me give you some examples first.

You know what's rare? A person getting dressed in workout clothes, going to the gym, walking in the front door, and then turning around to go home. I have a 100% success rate of exercising when I walk into a gym. I always do *something*. Why is it so rare to fail in that scenario? This is activity *before I've done one second of exercise,* and yet it has worked 100% of the time. That's because it's *real* short-term momentum. That momentum isn't based on how someone thinks they're doing, or how they did yesterday, it's based on taking several actual steps towards the gym! Each stage of the process carries real momentum and flows to the next step. That's why, for a long time, my only aim was to "show up" at the gym. I knew what would happen after that.

You know what else is rare? A person going to the gym daily for five years and then stopping. Why is that? It's *real* long-term momentum based on an exercise habit. I've been working out consistently for nine years now, and I'm in the top 10% of lazy people in the world.

It's painfully *common* for someone to try something for 30 days and stop then (or sooner). It's painfully *common* for someone to set a long-term goal and quit after two weeks. We've all done it. The excuses are endless, aren't they? But when you dig deeper, you see the issue—goals die when momentum dies, and that happens when you treat perceived momentum as real momentum.

Perceived Momentum Still Matters
Okay, now that I've bashed it, let me unbash it a bit.

Perceived momentum can be extremely useful. In the same way that a basketball player's belief they're "on fire" can turn into a brilliant performance, perceived momentum can do the same for us. It can even carry us through the momentum dead zone *sometimes*.

What's the issue, then? We want excellent results. We want confidence. Well, you can feed off of them when they're there! This is a matter of your core perspective, which will be revealed when you have an off day.

Seek to develop a nuanced perspective of how momentum works. It's critical to understand that there *is* value in perceived momentum (or confidence) in the mid-term, but that it's quite detrimental *if relied upon for continued action*.

When you understand the underlying mechanisms for human momentum in the short and long term and that mid-term momentum is more of a placebo effect or confidence boost than a lasting solution, your entire approach to life changes.

How Most Goals Are Anti-Momentum

Imagine if a team of basketball players believed fully in the "on fire" effect as the best way to make shots and win games. Rather than practice their shooting mechanics, they would go into every game believing or hoping that they'll "catch fire." But any evidence that they are "off" would crush their confidence. That's guaranteed to be a terrible, inconsistent basketball team!

Most people, when they attempt a goal, act like that basketball team. They rely *wholly* on perceived momentum. Using actual popular marketing language from other books, these short-term programs try to "kickstart" people to do something—eat better, work out more, vacuum, lose weight, work harder, and so on. Kickstart means "feed off of early results." It works until it (suddenly) doesn't. It's a gross misunderstanding of human behavior, psychology, and momentum. But hey, it sounds exciting and sells books, so people will keep writing about it.

Isn't it odd that people design programs to self-destruct? These programs often do two things that destroy short- and long-term momentum:

1. They encourage difficult goals; things like super-clean eating or 100 push-ups a day or brutal workout programs or high word-count writing sessions. Great ideas, but poor structure for momentum. Remember, goals are like pole vaulting. You must clear that number to win. You don't want to aim for 100 pushups and do 85; even though 85 push-ups is great, you failed to get over the bar. Because of this structure, the two most likely numbers you'll get are 100 or 0. You'll get 0 any time you don't think you can get all 100.

All-or-nothing thinking is the enemy of short-term

momentum because just to begin something means you must do it *all*. Sometimes, you won't want to begin a daunting task, and that's when you get nothing (the enemy of progress and success).

Every step forward creates **short-term momentum**, which is why it's always more valuable to *begin* (choose your direction) than to commit to something grand (and risk motionlessness). If you want to set lofty goals *after* you begin moving, that's fine because you've already established your direction with momentum.

2. They don't intend for you to do these things for long enough to change your brain. Again, there's zero scientific evidence for habits forming in 30 days. People are obsessed with that number! Since these usually end within 30 days, they can't generate **long-term momentum**. As I discussed in *Mini Habits*, the one study we've got on habit formation found a range of 18–254 days, with an average of 66 days.[4] Habits are a behavioral spectrum of familiarity, goodwill, and trust, not a magic number you need to hit.

Everything we've discussed explains why the structure of speed-based goals is *anti-momentum*. They slow you down and fail over time. Meanwhile, my stupid one push-up per day goal has endured and evolved into a consistent (full) exercise habit *nine years later*. It gave me an easy way to generate short- and long-term momentum. That's it. Nine years of working out is the predictable result of such an approach, but isn't it remarkable that it came from such a humble beginning? That's the magic of momentum![5]

The Rut Test

If you still think that you can ride a 30-day challenge into greatness, there's another issue with it you should consider. It is something everyone will face, regardless of their strategy.

Since mid-term goals and challenges rely on perception over your power to create momentum, they fail the rut test.[6]

What happens when (not if) you perceive your momentum to be negative or to have decreased? What happens when (not if) you perceive yourself to be in a rut? If you're relying on perception, you'll reinforce the rut.

This is the mistake people make. They allow themselves to rise and fall with their perception of their situation. But ruts are only held up by the idea that they exist. Let me explain.

Let's say that you have been making mistakes and not following your dreams for too long. From this position, you have a choice. You can believe in the power of the rut to keep you down or believe in your power to get out of it.

Those are the only two things that can happen.

The very second a person generates positive momentum, technically speaking, they're no longer in a rut (short term). They may have more work to do if the rut behavior is habitual (long term), but the way out is the same—keep creating positive momentum every day.

For example, let's say you feel like or perceive yourself to be in an unhealthy rut, where you don't exercise and eat unhealthy foods. What actual barrier besides your mind is preventing you from making your next meal a healthy one? What actual barrier is preventing you from taking a walk, lifting weights, or going on a run today? Right now?

I'm not talking about the weight of the entire change you want to make, I'm talking about ONE time. What can stop you? Only ideas that changes will be harder than they really are, that you need a perfect plan to even begin, that one healthy meal isn't enough, that the change you want to make will be too difficult, or that you'll never do or be enough. **Only the way you perceive your situation can create and sustain these kinds of ruts.**

This is the devastating damage of thinking in terms of results and numbers of successful days. *It drives us into an over-reliance on our perception of where we are.* It keeps us from easy steps that can generate real momentum and put us on a better path.

* * *

Right now, if you exercise and eat a healthy meal afterwards, what does that mean for your unhealthy rut? It means there is no rut at the moment. How can you be in a rut if you are currently standing victoriously on a mountaintop? Ruts are all in the mind because we have power to get out of them with real-world action and momentum.

Do you see how perceived momentum, whether positive or negative (based on feelings and results), can damage us?

- Positive perceived momentum too often is given priority over *real* momentum. This results in *superficial progress* that only lasts as long as your perception, which can collapse for any reason without warning.
- Negative perceived momentum holds us back artificially. It's like a person seeing a perilous cliff in front of them, when in reality it's a nice sidewalk with a lemonade stand nearby. They could walk forward easily, but they don't do it because the illusion of what it takes and means to move forward intimidates them.

The role of perceived momentum is clear. Use it and benefit from it when it's positive, but n*ever* depend on it again, because it can leave as fast as it arrives.

* * *

To put this in a real world example, I may *think* that I've written all I could for today and perceive that my momentum and creative energy are too low to continue. Right after that, I could set a small target to write one more sentence or paragraph to generate real momentum. TEST IT. I've been in this exact situation many times, and, more often than not, I've found my perceived loss of momentum was a total fabrication of my mind.

On the day that I wrote this sentence, I perceived myself to be in the biggest writing rut that I've been in for years. Despite my feelings, I started writing, having no confidence that I'd be able to write more than a paragraph. Six hours later, I was still writing. That's a writer on fire!

Perception is often wrong, especially in regards to momentum. You will always have some kind of perception of where you are at. But as long as you rely on generating real momentum over following your perception, you will shatter most negative perceptions (as I did today) and ride the waves of positive perception as long as they last without the crash.

The reason for my writing rut was everything I've warned against. In my prior two writing sessions, I got distracted, had no good ideas, and stared at the page instead of writing. **I let my perception of the last few days affect my willingness to show up the next day, as if it meant something.** I let it stop me from generating real momentum. And today, I saw the cost of that. The six-hour writing session was waiting for me for several days but I was afraid to try because I thought I was in a rut.

Neither you nor I will ever apply this perfectly. That's okay. The important thing is to know how momentum works and practice creating it as much as you can. The more you practice, the more consistent you'll be. It will take time to habitually move away from perception into real momentum. It will also be worth it!

Is Technology to Blame?

The lust for fast results and the hope that perceived momentum can power us directly to the top of our proverbial mountaintop must come from somewhere. Most of the self-help literature out there certainly doesn't help. But I think there could be a modern technological component to this.

Technology can make people impatient. I just counted that I only have to touch my phone *three times* in the Chipotle app to have a burrito bowl delivered to my door in 30 minutes. In less than ten seconds, I can look up how fast a great white shark swims (35 MPH, *shudder*). By design, modern societies give us what we want instantly or close to it. But since we aren't bionic yet, we still have to abide by our old-fashioned, slow-moving brain system.

One-week programs to "kickstart" your weight loss

journey sound like the fun, *fast,* exciting, high-tech solution! But nope, most are a poorly designed, slow, *anti-momentum mess.*

Perceived momentum is great, really, but it's also extremely fragile, dead the moment you *perceive it* to be dead. If you feel tired one day and miss the mark? Dead. If your results are uninspiring and you wonder if it's worth the work? Dead. If you're not feeling you can put in quality time or effort today? Dead.

The good news is, of course, that having a few bad days in a row doesn't mean you're doomed. It only means you haven't chosen to generate short-term momentum lately or that the momentum you generated was weaker than you wanted. You can try again today.

Real momentum is like a boulder tumbling down a mountain. The boulder doesn't care what you perceive it to be doing. *It's going down and won't stop for questions.* Perceived momentum is more like a CGI boulder running on Windows ME.

Golden Nugget: Seek Momentum Daily

Here is the golden nugget that I want to share with you. If you thought my whole spiel about real and perceived momentum was a "show" without substance, listen to this. This golden nugget pinpoints how you can apply this in your life, starting now.

Take this with you wherever you go, and you will be nearly unstoppable.

Until you build long-term momentum, which takes months to years, the onus is on you to create short-term momentum <u>every individual day</u> in areas that matter to you. That means moving in your chosen direction, even if you can only manage one step forward.

I can't stress enough how useful this sentiment is! The chief reason people fail at anything is that they take real momentum for granted or assume they have it before they do. People think doing something for a week or a month straight means they can "coast." No, no, no. They haven't built long-term momentum yet (and even long-term momentum isn't infallible, but it's strong and the best we can do).

Generate short-term momentum every day as if it's day one. This is easy to do, as we will discuss in Part Two. Over time, your results will be as magical as sparkling snow on Christmas Day.

If you apply this golden nugget, you will end up in a vortex of positive momentum. For starters, you will get skilled at generating short-term positive momentum, the applications of which are innumerable! And second, all the areas you generate momentum for will pay long-term dividends.

Principle 4
Everything You Do Ripples Exponentially

We've covered the fundamentals of momentum. We know how it works short term and long term, and we know to avoid the pitfalls of perceived momentum. Now it's time to look at the exciting stuff. We're moving from how it works to what it can do for us.

In the 4th and final principle, we will explore the math of momentum, but it's more exciting than most math. Human momentum isn't a linear force but an exponential one. For every bit of momentum you create, it creates several more baby momentum bits, which can create their own babies, making your original momentum a grandma.

Amateurs and Grandmasters: The Difference
One key difference between amateur and grandmaster chess players is that amateurs (me) only think about their

next move or three; Grandmaster Magnus Carlsen sometimes thinks 15 to 20 moves ahead. (His brain must weigh 50 pounds.) What if we thought that way about our actions?

Every action has momentum-shifting properties that will affect *your next several actions*, which have their own momentum to affect further actions. When considering action, unsuccessful people think like amateur chess players, focusing only on the initial impact of an action. Successful doers think like grandmaster chess players, because they consider the many ripples of momentum an action will create now and later and how that might affect their goals and dreams.[1]

In my book, *Mini Habits for Weight Loss*, I included one of my favorite quotes of all time. It discusses the complex interactions between food, energy, and biology, showing how one small action can ripple exponentially in one system.

"What you eat actually changes how you expend energy. Similarly, how you expend energy changes what (and how) you eat. To be even more nuanced, what you eat further impacts what you subsequently eat. As you increase (or decrease) in size, this impacts how you expend energy."[2]
~ Peter Attia, MD

* * *

People often oversimplify weight change to calories eaten and expended. But that cannot account for a person's neuropsychology (the relationship of behavior to the brain's processes), their relationship with food, and crucial psychobiological interactions (the relationship of behavior to biological processes). Case in point: When a person loses a lot of weight from semi-starvation (the typical dieter), their body fights back. Small details matter because they can ripple.

Ripplestiltskin

We believe that a large-diameter ripple can come from a small object hitting the water because we've seen the entire process play out quickly in real time. In life, such ripples of momentum also exist, but they are invisible and play out in different behaviors across many currents of time, making them much harder to see and believe than acorn-made ripples.

The ripple effect is hard to foresee or believe before and as it happens, and impossible to deny in hindsight.

It will be useful to specify the different exponential momentum ripples. That will make them easier to predict and see. We've already covered the first two.

The Ripples of Momentum

There are three "ripples" of momentum to consider with every action you take: the near term, the long term, and adjacent areas.

The order you see in this image isn't important or correct in every case. Adjacent areas might be the next "ripple" to come after the near term, or it might come after seven years of long-term progress in an area. The order isn't as important as knowing the three.

Since we've covered the power of near-term and long-term momentum, let's talk about that last ripple. The "adjacent areas" ripple is powerful beyond measure.

Adjacent Areas

Every action "ripples" to create other thoughts, feelings, effects, and actions, which themselves can ripple!

I've only recently realized how important basketball is in my life. It's just a game, a sport, but the momentum basketball generates in adjacent areas of my life is *astronomical*. It genuinely astonishes me how much it affects my life. When I play basketball, I'm also…

- Reducing stress
- Improving my health
- Getting fit
- Socializing
- Making acquaintances or friends
- Gaining self-confidence
- Sleeping much better

Each of those areas has its own set of short-term momentum, long-term momentum, and adjacent area momentum. That's impossible to quantify, so let's just look at one example, which is improved sleep.

Sometimes, I have trouble sleeping deeply and will awaken groggy even after sleeping for 8–10 hours. But when I play basketball for a couple of hours, I've noticed I sleep like a puma that night and wake up earlier than usual the next morning, feeling refreshed and well rested. (Pumas sleep very well because they are cats and cats invented sleep.) In short, the effect basketball has on one adjacent area, sleep, is *miraculous*.

Now, to explore just one adjacent area of *that adjacent area*, consider the impact of waking up earlier with more energy vs waking up later with fatigue. That difference can't be quantified—it affects *everything else* I do! More efficient sleep gives me up to an extra hour per day. This is just *one* adjacent area of *one* adjacent area of playing basketball, and the conclusion is: "too impactful to comprehend." How can I fathom the whole impact of playing basketball if I can't even quantify one ripple of one ripple? This is looking like HVS3.

Playing basketball (or anything else) is not an isolated event. When I choose to do it, I'm enriching my life on a lot of levels, many of which I'm not consciously aware of (such as increased blood flow, nutrient distribution, and other internal cellular processes). Like anything exponential, it quickly becomes too massive for anyone to wrap their mind around. Follow one tangent (of many) and you'll practically never run out of cascading adjacent areas.

Play Basketball > Better Sleep > More Energy > Wake up

Earlier > Feel Better about Myself/No Sleep-in Guilt > More Assertive > Conquer World > Infinity Stones > Snap Thanos Away > Marry Scarlet Witch > Bachelor Party with Captain America and Iron Man

I admit that playing basketball (probably) won't get me into the Marvel Cinematic Universe, but pick any of those real points prior to that fictional detour and you'll find several adjacent areas that *they* affect. How might being more assertive help my dating life or business? How might improvements in *those* areas affect other areas of my life?

If you try to see all the ripples of one action and the ripples of those ripples rippling into rippled ripples, it's like trying to comprehend the size of the universe or the number of grains of sand in the world. The potential momentum of just one action is on *that* level. It's only hard to see it because our lives are made of *so many actions.*

Some actions benefit us, others hurt us, and many are a mixture of help and harm. This mixture produces what we know as our life, and the complexity of all the variables shrouds the incredible power of each individual action, just as the ripple from one acorn is nearly impossible to see in rough waters with dozens of other acorns dropping in.

Putting the Pieces Together

Let's look at some specific examples that show us the entire framework of momentum.

When you exercise...

1. You are much more likely to continue exercising than stop (near term).
2. You're more likely to exercise in the future (long term).
3. Exercise can help you sleep better, improve your mood, and increase your self-esteem (adjacent).
4. Every affected adjacent area has its own momentum chain. For example, with exercise, your mood is likely to improve in the short term and long term, and your good mood may make someone else's day. This is a true story: One day, a man paid for the car behind him at a drive thru. Little did he know, that man was planning to end his life that day. The unexpected act of kindness changed the suicidal stranger's mind, and he decided to keep living and make others' lives better (exponential adjacent).[3]

When you do heroin...

1. You're much more likely to continue using heroin than stop (near term).
2. You're more likely to use heroin in the future (long term).
3. Heroin can cause several horrible side effects, make you unemployable, and even kill you (adjacent).
4. Every affected adjacent area has its own momentum chain. For example, being unemployed makes it harder to

get a job now and later, which may cause homelessness and desperation. Drug addiction also puts tremendous strain on medical facilities and families (exponential adjacent).

When you practice guitar…

1. You're much more likely to continue practicing guitar than stop (near term).
2. You're more likely to practice guitar and other musical instruments in the future (long term).
3. You'll improve your finger dexterity and strength, lower your stress levels, boost your mood, and gain music knowledge (adjacent).
4. Every affected adjacent area has its own momentum chain. For example, playing guitar may give you increased confidence, which results in a relationship, which results in becoming a parent (exponential adjacent). It's not as crazy as it sounds! Many babies have been born because of pleasant music.

Every action has three types of momentum, with the potential to unleash an exponential chain reaction on your life. Knowing this, prospective actions look *nothing* like they used to look, do they? They carry a certain *weight*, not based on their size but based on their potential to ripple into destruction or glory.

And to be clear, this isn't theory. You can verify the truth of what I'm saying right now, because *it has already happened in your life.* Think about your worst mistakes or best accomplishments in life.

Let's start with the bad. Your worst mistakes will be traceable to small choices and actions that snowballed out of control.

Negative Outcomes from Small Beginnings

- The small choice to spend time with a certain person
- The small choice to neglect an area of your life
- The small choice to try something dangerous "just this once"
- The small choice to give this person "one more chance"
- The small choice to ignore a subtle but clear red flag (This one cost me $5,000 recently, which I now can't compound in a better investment. Ouch!)

Your triumphs will be traceable to seemingly insignificant actions that snowballed into amazing opportunities or results. This goes for personal stories and companies. Every massive corporation has a humble origin story. Some companies were unplanned altogether (Apple).

Positive Outcomes from Small Beginnings

- The small choice to do one push-up every day (or

any other mini habit)
- The small choice to spend time with an uplifting or wise person
- The small choice to put yourself out there and take a smart risk
- The small choice to make an appointment with a therapist
- The small choice to apply for a job, create a minimum viable product, or try a new side business
- The small choice to meditate, write, read books like this one, or practice a skill

My greatest accomplishment so far in life has been the impact and success of my books. They are now in over 20 languages and have helped hundreds of thousands of people (myself included) live better. That path started with me buying the domain name deepexistence.com for $10 on a "sure, why not?" whim, which only happened because I read a blog about blogging, which happened because I read a book on a whim that got me interested in personal development (*Getting Things Done* by David Allen), which got me interested in writing as a way to explore it. And, trust me, this is not even the smallest part of the chain, but I'll spare you the minute details.

The chain of events ending with my books being read in 20+ languages started because I was slightly disorganized in college and wanted to see if I could improve it by reading a book. It's *embarrassing* how casual and insignificant the inciting actions for my greatest successes have been. But that's how it always is!

Love Stories

When people first meet their spouse, it's a monumental moment that will change the entire course of their lives. And while the "story" is often funny or interesting, that's because of how *weird and offhand* it is compared to what it means.

I'm not married yet, but I met one ex-girlfriend at a party. They had one of those giant bouncy balls, and before we had spoken a single word to each other, I kicked the bouncy ball. It hit her in the face. Yep. Smooth move, Stephen. I apologized profusely, of course, and we started talking. We dated for a year and I learned a lot in that relationship. The bouncy-ball-to-the-face move works every time, guys.

Some of my life-changing actions include kicking a bouncy ball, buying a book on a whim, and doing one push-up. We can do great things with the most unimpressive actions.

There is, however, a key difference between kicking a bouncy ball into a woman's face and doing one push-up a day. One is accidental and the other is intentional (I would never do a push-up intentionally). Big things will happen in our lives regardless of what we do. *But if we live with intention and know of the power of momentum, we can intentionally turn easy and small wins into massive wins.*

Golden nugget: The smallest action can bring people out of a seemingly insurmountable struggle if it triggers a reversal in momentum.

Climbing the Dam Wall

There is a famous video on YouTube with over 166 million views of ibexes climbing a dam wall. The wall is nearly vertical but textured. If the dam were completely smooth, these animals would have no chance of climbing it. But, with textured rocks sticking out mere millimeters, the ibex can use its sharp, concave hooves to gain enough footing to climb up and down.[4]

* * *

If we are ibexes and the top of the dam represents reaching our life goals, think of momentum as the small ridges in the dam that enable us to scale the wall. It's an incredible feat only made possible by the subtlest textures. You'll look back and think, "Wow, how did I get all the way up here with those measly ridges? It's... magic."

We think of powerful things as being easy to spot—you know, obvious and dramatic—but momentum in human lives is barely perceptible most of the time, like acorn ripples in rough waters or dam wall textures. It's a subtle, steady power that can lead us to gargantuan feats.

To put it as a 7th grader in the 1970s might put it, so far we've established that momentum is totally rad, important, and life-changing. We've also touched on the fact that we can generate it more easily than one might think and that it usually begins subtly and unimpressively.

In the next chapter, we're going to examine some forces that affect momentum. The more we can understand the specific ways that momentum is generated, sustained, stopped, and reversed in our lives, the better we can control it. But first, a short bonus section.

Bonus: The Proficiency Cycle

Proficiency makes momentum compound like so: The better you get at something, the more appealing it is. The more appealing it is, the more you'll do it. The more you do it, the more proficient you'll become, which restarts the cycle.

If you think about some of the most successful people in different areas, they all seem to have gotten into this virtuous cycle of proficiency. Tiger Woods was so good at golf that he gained all the fame and recognition that one could want in a lifetime and then some. What do you think that made him want to do? Play more golf!

* * *

Tiger could have tried that classic transition from pro golfer to pro Scrabble player. He could have read the dictionary every night and memorized weird two-letter words like "qi." Curiously, he kept playing golf, despite the millions of dollars, admiration, and satisfying use of skill the sport offered him. Oh wait, that sounds pretty nice. It makes sense that he's played 25 years of golf professionally at the time of writing (his pro career started at 20 years old in August 1996).

Greater proficiency in an area generates increasingly greater rewards. And these rewards include the satisfaction you gain from being proficient.

The Satisfaction of Work

Humans desire to be useful. Retirement can be excruciating for some—you go from contributing to a company, to your family, or to society to spending your days golfing (non-professionally?) and watching TV. That's fine if you want to live that way—no judgement from this lazy author—but the transition doesn't sit well with everyone.

I'm the last person you'd expect to hear this from, but I don't plan to retire. I love the retirement lifestyle and I already emulate it in some ways.[5] I always prefer play over work, and my "lazy side" is 85% of my body. But I find great satisfaction in creative work, especially as I get better at it.

* * *

Proficiency is an endless well of satisfaction. The principles of momentum are how you get proficient, but we'll discuss more specific momentum-building tactics later in the book.

"True happiness comes from the joy of deeds well done, the zest of creating things new."
~ Antoine de Saint-Exupéry

Chapter 5
Environment, Effort, and Momentum

A car moves when the force produced by its engine overcomes other forces, such as friction and wind. What if the car is upside down at the bottom of a mountain? Then its wheels can't grip the ground, and, even if they could, it would struggle to ascend a steep mountain. As in physics, human momentum is determined by competing forces. The strongest forces determine the direction of our momentum.

The first principle of momentum, *you're most likely to do what you just did*, **can succumb to a counteractive environment.**

If I take one step forward, another step is likely in most cases. But if I take a step up a wall, I'm *not* likely to take another step (unless I'm wearing gravity boots or have ibex skills). Environment doesn't invalidate momentum's principles, but it can act as gatekeeper in extreme circumstances.

Have you heard of exercise-induced urticaria? While society champions exercise as a worthwhile pursuit, people with this condition are *allergic* to it, experiencing typical allergic reactions such as hives. Some are so allergic that exercise can even cause life-threatening anaphylaxis. You can't build momentum in something that will kill you if you succeed.

Your environment can make momentum and success difficult. (It's rarely impossible like in the case of exercise-induced urticaria.) Part of success is in recognizing and avoiding, fleeing, or changing negative environments, and then seeking an environment that actively helps you.

Environment Can Make Success Easier Too

Imagine a large boulder resting atop a hill. Whether you nudge the boulder or punch it with great effort, the environment will overshadow the difference in applied force—it's atop a hill! *Any amount of force that tips the boulder down the slope will produce massive momentum as gravity gets hold of it.*

* * *

The Magic of Momentum

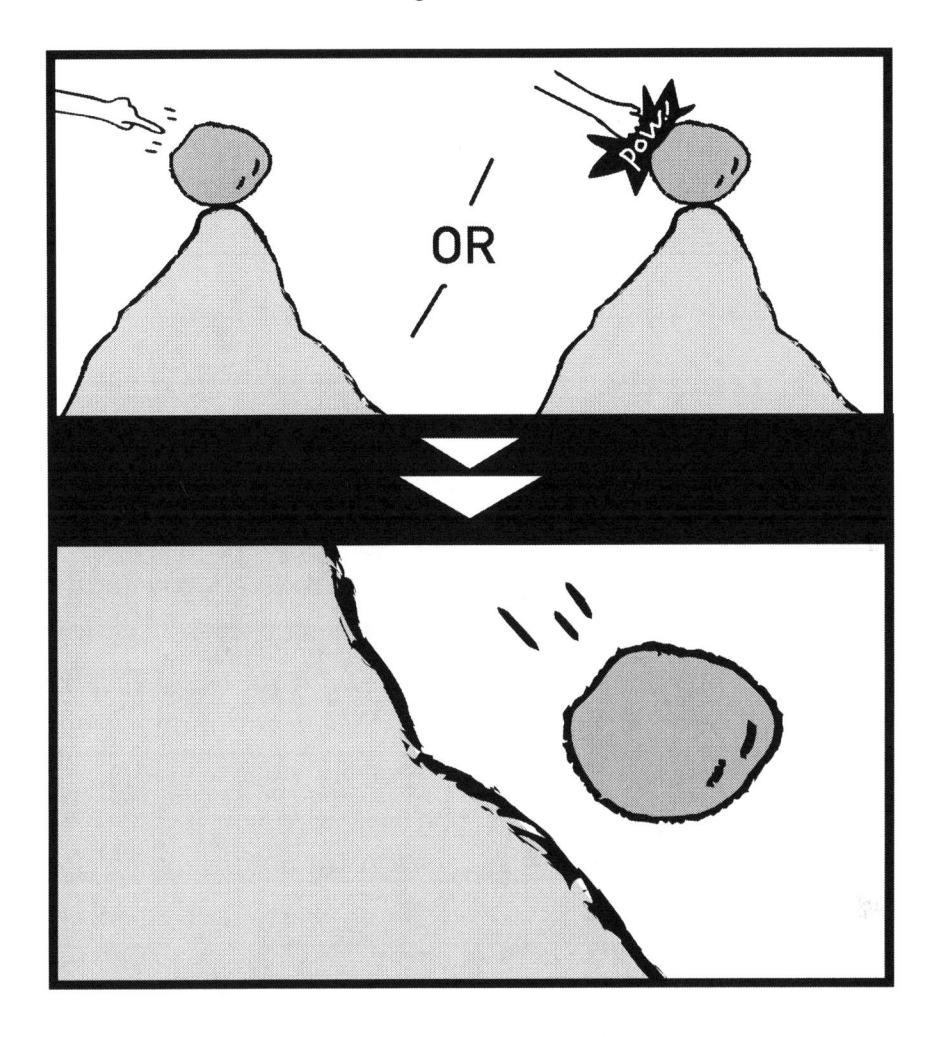

When your environment does much of the work for you, a minor effort can generate a result equal to that of a big effort. You just need to show up.

Environment isn't merely physical but mental as well. Consider the mental environment that whatever "system" you use creates. A harsh, judgmental diet system shames you for eating a small piece of candy, creating a "don't mess up" or "walking on thin ice" type of environment with your food choices. A process-focused and less demanding system, however, feels relaxed and empowers you. Instead of having to be perfect, what if you were asked to merely nudge boulders atop mountains? The perspective and method you choose make a big difference!

Immovable Boulders

A heavy boulder at the bottom of a mountain is all but impossible to move without serious equipment. If your effort is futile, what's the point of trying at all? There may not be a point. Those who start and stop goals constantly know the feeling all too well. It's better to try something else or perhaps *somewhere* else. At some point, everyone will try to change something that their environment will not allow to change.

Example 1: You can be the best communicator in the world, the most thoughtful person, loyal, and perfect overall, putting 100% loving effort towards a successful relationship. If you're with the wrong person, perhaps someone not willing to invest in the relationship, the relationship will still fail.

Example 2: Say that you want to lose weight and get fit. You try working out two hours a day. If your diet remains pizza and beer, you will still struggle to lose weight, even if you can sustain grueling workouts. Exercise cannot bring significant results within the pizza diet environment (unless you have crazy genes and youth on your side). You might commit to eating healthier, but if your house is full of *unhealthy* food, you will probably fail because of constant temptation for accessible snacks.

Positive changes are hard enough to make on their own. When you also must fight a poor environment, the odds are stacked against you. Conversely, if big results are an easy step forward because your environment is *conducive* to that (the boulder atop a hill), it will encourage you to take action and succeed, often because you can see and experience that even minimal effort makes a big difference. A positive environment can turn small to moderate effort into colossal success.

The closer to neutral an environment is, the less it matters and the more important other forces are for results. We want neutral-to-positive environments for our desired lifestyle.

Changing Your Environment

At the gym, I explained to another player that I gained 10 pounds because of the pandemic. I couldn't play full court basketball during lockdown, and that had been my lifelong favorite source of aerobic exercise. Sure, I tried running around the block, but even a few minutes of running feels like work (bottom of the mountain), whereas two hours of basketball is effortless fun (top of the mountain). In addition, my home environment became a bit... beer heavy. More on that later.

On the bright side, I worked out frequently at my home gym during the pandemic, and my effort there was actually greater than before. But my effort at home returned maybe 1/3 of the results that it would have at the gym, because one had a lifetime of momentum behind it and the other was a new style of exercise. When I played basketball, it would often be for two hours. My home gym workouts were frequent, but not as effortless, long, or intense.

These days, I get better results in my home gym with less effort than before. I've made it more appealing with better equipment and a TV for watching sports; I have also gained familiarity with it over the last couple of years. It took me a while to build that kind of environment and momentum, but it's well worth it now!

When I told the basketball player I gained weight, he said, "Only 10? I gained 60 pounds." The pandemic created a drastic environmental shift for most people (quarantine). Unlike my initial experience and the experience of this other player, another friend did better than ever exercising in the pandemic because she had more time for home workouts. The point isn't that quarantine is always bad, it's that environment influences our results, and we should note how it does in each case and adjust as necessary.

* * *

Basic positive environment ideas:

- A cleaner home creates less stress and more clarity.
- Ergonomic desk setups create less pain and may help avoid chronic tendon injuries such as carpel tunnel syndrome.
- Light color and intensity can impact your mood, energy level, and hormones. For example, with Phillips Hue color bulbs, my home lights automatically turn red after sunset. Why red? Because blue light delays the release of melatonin, which can disrupt your sleep, and red has no such drawback.
- Candles/incense, art, calendars, roommates, air temperature, music, layout, furniture, and so on can impact your mood and behavior.

Do your best to create an environment that makes it easier to live your ideal life. Once you've created a neutral or better environment, there's just one thing left to do. Nudge that boulder. Not think about nudging it. Not feel like nudging it. Just... nudge it.

Thoughts, Actions, Feelings: The Triad of the Human Experience

"Action may not always bring happiness, but there is no happiness without action."

— Benjamin Disraeli

Ah, the human experience. It's great. It's awful. It depends on who (and when) you ask. For all the things that life can be, we can break our experience down into three parts.

We think.
We feel.
We act.

We experience the world through thought, emotion, and action (not necessarily in that order). Our power is to decide how we will command this system to our greatest benefit. There are many considerations here, from cycles to chain reactions. But let's start off with these six important facts.

How we think affects how we act.
How we think affects how we feel.
How we feel affects how we think.
How we feel affects how we act.
How we act affects how we think.
How we act affects how we feel.

* * *

```
         ACTIONS
           ●
          ↗ ↖
         ↙   ↘
   ●           ●
THOUGHTS ←→ FEELINGS
```

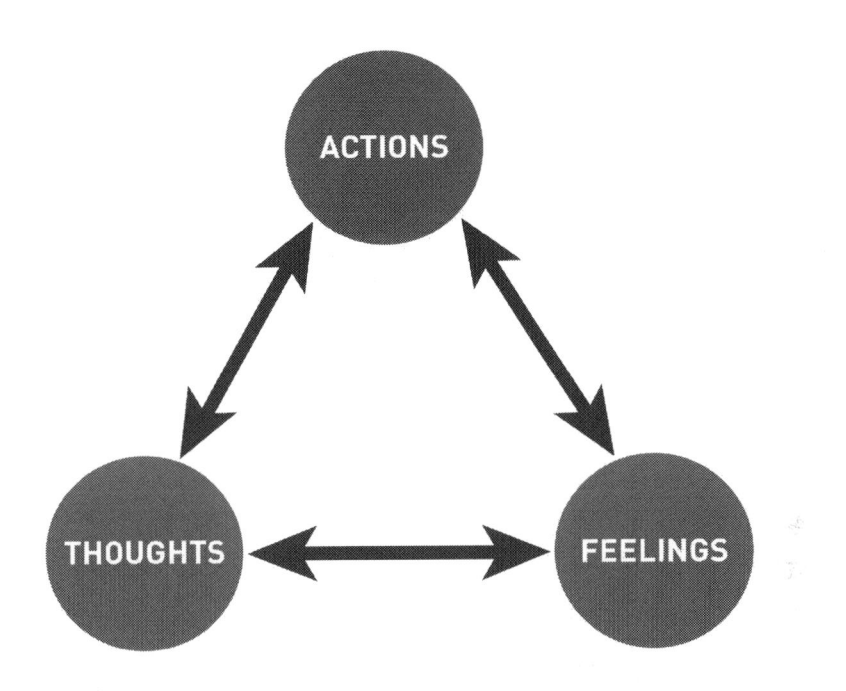

More concisely, everything affects everything. Whichever tip of this triangle we decide to focus on *will* have some impact on the other two. The question isn't about what "works." You can get results by improving any of these areas because each of them carries momentum and affects the other two. *But we need to know which one works best as the catalyst for the greatest change. That's action.*

Action supersedes thoughts and feelings for one reason—it is objective and they are subjective. For example, if you think you aren't a golfer and yet you golf every day, guess what? You're still a golfer! What if you feel you aren't a golfer? Sorry, but you're a golfer if, you know, you *golf*. Golfers golf. Sooner than later, you're going to think and feel that you are a golfer too.

Action wins because it isn't debatable. Thoughts and feelings have spikes of prominence in our lives, but the actions we [don't] take always wind up dominating our thoughts, feelings, and life trajectory in time. Thoughts and feelings can affect action as well, and they can be powerful enough to derail us, but if you want to make a positive change in your life, leading with action will bring you the best results.

There may be cases in which thoughts and feelings significantly (and negatively) affect a person's life. But the solution is not any different. People run into problems when they allow their thoughts and feelings to take precedence over action. If you have problems with thoughts and feelings, the solution is usually action, the wellspring of life. What's more damaging than negative thoughts or feelings? Inaction.

We need to prioritize action, but in a smart way. We know action requires energy, but it also requires energy to figure out what actions to take and when. If you don't have a system for managing this, you may find yourself drained of energy before you even begin! How can we address this? With passive productivity systems.

Save Energy: Use a Passive Productivity System

Productivity is "achieving or producing a significant amount or result." But the pressure to be "productive" can be toxic. This comes from a narrow view of life and what excellence means. For example, if you produce 50% more content or money than before but end up with poor mental health, that's part productive and part unproductive. You produced more but, in doing so, you got a *significantly negative result* of poor mental health.

Thus, productivity is not just numbers and milestones. Productivity must also include quality of life, rest, and even joy. In other words, we must strive to produce content, money, and progress *simultaneously with* greater quality of life, health, and joy.

True productivity is not maximizing your energy, it's managing your energy. If your only goal is to *maximize* your energy, you will, counterintuitively, fail to do so. It's much like successful weight loss—a study found that participants who tried to lose weight fared worse than those who simply tried to maintain their weight.[1] When you attempt to maximize your energy, blind aggression prevents you from seeing the threat of a forced move backwards.

Burnout, an increasingly common problem in the workplace, is a forced move backwards in which people become physically and/or mentally sick from overworking. Those who suffer clinical burnout are often forced to take weeks off of work. That's not ideal or productive.

When you *manage* your energy, it means you desire to move forward while respecting your human need for rest, fun, and play. If someone struggles with productivity, they probably don't manage their energy well. They either don't use enough of it (resulting in lethargy) or use too much of it (resulting in burnout).

If you plan out your entire life in advance, your greatest risk is burnout. If you plan out none of your life in advance, your greatest risk is stagnancy. If you have a system that lets you plan some and adapt to circumstances, you have a great chance to manage your energy well for sustainable, enjoyable productivity.

Why Passive Systems Are Best for Productivity

A productivity system is something you use to manage the non-scheduled aspects of your life. What do you do after work? You need to decide whether to play with your dog, learn a new language, write a story, or to start a side business in your free time. These unscheduled areas offer some of the most satisfying, useful, and meaningful opportunities in life.

If you were perfectly productive, you'd be like a train. Trains are several times more fuel efficient than highway trucks for moving cargo, and it's all about the tracks. Train tracks passively guide the locomotive in the right direction at all times. Excess energy pushes the train the only way it can go, which is forward. In the same way, after your non-negotiable activities, a passive productivity system will push you forward instead of being wasted in the wrong direction.

If you don't have some way of directing your energy passively (like train tracks do for a train), you'll spend too much of your energy *deciding on and managing tasks* instead of doing them and reaping the rewards. Micromanaging tasks is exhausting work for little reward. It's better to spend your energy on completing tasks than managing tasks! So, while it's possible to be productive without a passive system, it's also 10x harder.

To be clear, no system is 100% passive because you must ultimately decide yourself what direction you go; passivity is more of a scale of how easy your system makes it for you to decide your direction and act on it. Using the train track example, an optimally passive system means you're able to put down tracks quickly and get your caboose moving!

The more passive the system, the less energy it takes for you to move forward into action.

You might wonder what a passive system looks like in practice. I'm about to show you the best one I have developed for myself. This is the latest result of several experimentations with building systems, and I'm not sure how I could improve it further. But before we get into it, let's cover some popular (less efficient) systems.

Commonly used productivity systems include the to-do list and the calendar. These are popular for good reason—they are relatively lightweight. Their main issues are:

They are not passive. They offer no guidance. To-do lists and calendars start out blank. You must think of the action and then write it down each day. Sometimes this is easy and sometimes it isn't. A big problem here is blind spots—you will probably select the first tasks that come to mind, right? That's good in a way—fast action beats excessive deliberation 93% of the time. But non-urgent tasks like your dream trip or organizing your closet may remain hidden in the back of your mind. You might forget about very important things (or never prioritize them) if you're only drawing from memory and current obvious needs.

They are rigid. What happens if you sprain your ankle on Tuesday? That will change the texture of your day on Wednesday. A pre-filled to-do list is now a mess on Wednesday because you must reconstruct it through a new lens of "sprained ankle." (A to-do list made the same day can avoid this issue.)

There are more complex systems you can use, such as

David Allen's *Getting Things Done*. Allen's system makes perfect sense in how it slices and dices your life up into digestible bits. It does a fantastic job of presenting your entire life to you, which solves problem #1 of calendars and to-do lists. But it is an extremely *active* system requiring daily maintenance. If you stop maintaining the system, it becomes useless.

Since I hate having to maintain a system and need a passive system to guide me without making me work for it, I created a zero-maintenance system. It requires no upkeep, no updating, and has no wasted movements. Despite being more robust and comprehensive, it's even faster to set up than making a to-do list every day!

The system I speak of is a magnetic whiteboard with magnetic dry erase labels. Here's what my board looks like. Please don't judge it based on my awful handwriting.

* * *

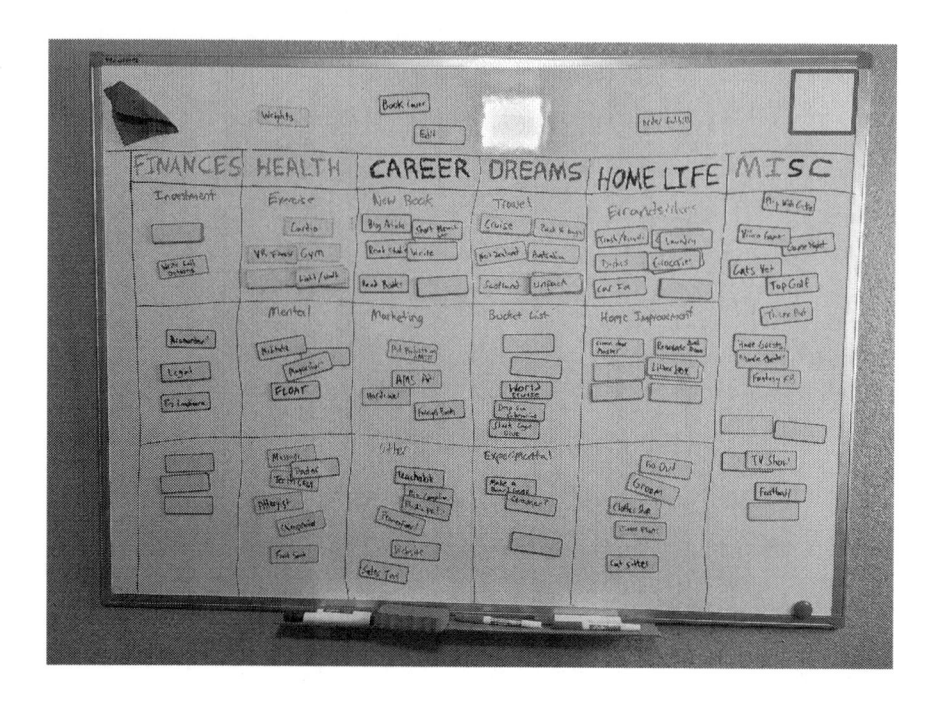

I've divided my life up into five different sections: finances, health, career, dreams, home life, and a misc section for everything else. There are subcategories within each of the major sections. At a glance, this helps me zoom in on a known activity quickly, or it lets me see all the options within a category if I think I should focus on that area of my life today.

Once I select a task to do, I simply move it vertically up the board to the top area, which serves as my "active to-do list" for the day. Once I complete an action, I move it back to its category below.

The Magnetic Life Management System (MLMS)
It helps to name things, so that you can talk about them or

reference them with others. For due diligence, I named this system and gave it an acronym. The MLMS has several advantages over other systems. Here are seven of my favorite ones!

1. I never have to *rewrite* common tasks, such as going to the gym, writing, fulfilling an online order, and so on. I simply grab the task's magnet and move it to the "active" area of the board. If you write a to-do list every day, that could mean rewriting common tasks *hundreds of times* per year—not a very efficient system! I only had to write "laundry" one time.

2. While the system is most useful for recurrent tasks, it has no issues with one-time tasks either. If I have a temporary task that I know I won't do again or for a long time (set up Christmas tree), I can simply write it on the whiteboard directly instead of using a magnetic label. Then I can erase it when I'm done.

3. It works as well for long-term projects and dreams as it does for daily chores like cleaning and laundry. They all exist within the same system but, as they are categorized, you never have to think about your dreams alongside dirty socks (unless you want to?). When you are ready to think about your dreams and how to make them happen, they are all right there in the same place!

4. I have larger dry erase magnets for multi-step projects. I

can fit several actions on one of these magnets, giving me a lot of flexibility in how I structure my to-do list. A recent example of this was before a trip to Greece. I had a lot of things to do and remember as I prepared to travel internationally, so I used a bigger magnet as a categorized Greece to-do list within my larger list of things to do. The list within a list concept is often messy and difficult to pull off with most types of software or productivity systems but, in this one, it's intuitive and easy.

5. Tasks remain categorized throughout the entire process. Digital productivity apps can do this, but it's a hassle for pen/paper to-do lists. Since the tasks in the MLMS move directly up the board, they are always vertically in line with their proper category, even when on the active to-do list. This can be very helpful, especially over time as you learn where the "exercise" magnets are—before you even read the activity, you know that you still need to work out in some capacity today just by seeing the magnet's location. The magnets I use are also color coded, which adds another layer of identification if you wish.

6. Changing your mind is as easy as swapping magnets. I may plan to play basketball at the local gym for my daily exercise and then change my mind and decide to do a weightlifting workout at home. Easy! I just switch the gym magnet with the weights magnet. No other system is faster or easier for activating and deactivating tasks.

* * *

7. Over time, this system "collects" all the different fragments of your life and makes you aware of them; it gives you a broad view of your life and all it entails. For example, it might be on the 3rd day that you realize you need to add a "groceries" magnet, and then it becomes a part of your system forever. As time goes on, you will get a clearer and clearer picture of your life.

8. Instead of having to think of everything on the spot every day, I have the luxury of drawing from a large pool of preselected valuable actions to take.

MLMS Downsides

The obvious downside—the system is not portable. It's on a wall in your home. If you work from home (as I do) or your home base is the primary place where you operate in a productive capacity, this works just fine. If you want to take your "list" with you on the road, simply take a picture of your board with your phone.

Other downsides of this system are the setup and cost. For the best results, it requires a rather large magnetic whiteboard. The one I use is four feet wide; I anchored it to my bedroom wall with included dry wall anchors (as of writing, these boards cost about $60 on Amazon). The magnets are also a little expensive ($17 for 40 of them, and I got two packs). Still, at just over $100 initial investment, it's been well worth it for a system I use every day.

* * *

You may end up partially erasing or fading your writing by picking up magnets and moving them around (you can still read them). It doesn't happen a lot, especially if you're careful to grab by the edges. It happens to me because I haphazardly throw my magnets around, but it rarely requires having to rewrite the task. If you want to avoid this issue and grab magnets with reckless abandon, you can use wet erase markers, which are erasable with water only.

As for my philosophy on phone productivity apps, I don't like them. My cell phone is a place of distraction, and every time I've tried a productivity app, I've abandoned it. Physical productivity tools are a respite from the digital world, safe from its many distractions!

The Magnetic Life Management System Is Always up to Date

My favorite aspect of this system is that, unlike most, it does not get out of date if you don't use it for a day, a week, or even months. For me, this is a requirement. My system must be able to handle some amount of neglect, because I will neglect the best system in the history of Earth at some point.

Mobile to-do apps badger you every day for tasks that aren't done, taunting you with a "late" label, requiring you to push them back a day or reschedule them or delete them. Even without such annoying notifications, leaving a task on your to-do list for days is easy to do and psychologically irritating. It's micromanaging at its worst, wasting your time and energy on menial tasks. And if you leave for vacation, any productivity apps you use are likely to be a veritable mess when you return.

If I go on a trip or have a day or two in which I don't do some tasks or ignore the system altogether, I simply reset the system by moving all the magnets down to the lower part of the board. There's no writing or rescheduling, just a 10-second reset and it's as good as new. The system serves me when and how I want it to, not the other way around.

Passive systems decrease the time and effort required for deliberation, which is incredibly empowering. Before you have an effective passive system like the MLMS to organize common tasks, just choosing what action to take can feel overwhelming. The MLMS is infinitely adaptable, too. Some days, I may only pick three primary tasks. On other days, I've picked 10+ tasks that I want or need to get done.

I'm not saying you must adopt this system, I just want to explain what's valuable about it. Ultimately, each person needs to find the right balance between comprehensiveness and simplicity. I think some people even enjoy the "busywork" required to organize and manage more complex systems, and that's completely fine. Find a system that works for you.

* * *

If there's one thing I've learned, it's that general productivity requires some kind of system. When the system is good enough, it will help you generate positive momentum. Poor productivity means you don't have a system or your system doesn't serve your needs. This isn't an issue of laziness. I'm both lazy and productive. Others aren't lazy and are still unproductive. It's the system.

Maybe you're like me, in which case anything that requires you to micromanage your life is a non-starter. Or maybe you're not, in which case more complex, active systems might be exactly what you need to feel empowered and fully organized. While I think that passive systems are inherently superior because they are lightweight, the only right system is the one that meshes with your personality and needs.

If you struggle with knowing what to do each day, it means that you haven't found the right system yet to organize your life.

The right productivity system can be more than just a way to manage your life. When I look at my whiteboard, I get *excited* because it fits my personality type. I have all of my options laid out for me, and I get to pick the exact ones that fit today, right now. There's no busywork or complicated procedures to go through. I move a magnet and that task becomes active. It's empowering!

***

When I tried the *Getting Things Done* (GTD) system by David Allen (twice, actually), I really liked some aspects of it. But, each time, it got to a point that I dreaded the steps I had to take every day just to keep it current. And I should note that the setup of that system requires quite a few purchases.

The GTD system itself is a daily task to maintain. I'm not talking about hours of work, but mere minutes a day. I'm lazier than most, so even 10 minutes a day to manage the system that manages my life was unacceptable in my mind. If you like the idea of a thorough system that incorporates almost every conceivable aspect of your life but requires daily maintenance, I recommend reading *Getting Things Done*. If you prefer something simpler, try out the MLMS or daily to-do lists.

For more information about the MLMS, including the specific products I use for my board, visit minihabits.com/momentum/

In this chapter, I've emphasized an "action-first" philosophy. Don't confuse that with effort. You do not necessarily need to try harder to get better results, and here's why.

Golden Nugget: Momentum Dominates Effort

Action is the way forward. So, we must give 110% effort and "take massive action" all day every day, right?! RIGHT?! LET'S GO!!!!!!

No.

There is a secret to life that I want to share with you. The entire book leads us to this point. If you remember only one thing from this book, this next sentence is a good choice.

Momentum matters more than effort.

Try to stop a runaway tractor trailer going down a mountain. Try *really* hard. Splat. Momentum matters more than effort.

***

Work 90 hours a week for minimum wage while a millionaire lounges in a beach chair with passive investments. The millionaire makes more money without trying. Momentum matters more than effort.

Try beating Tiger Woods in golf. Try beating LeBron James in basketball. In terms of effort, they play casually and you sweat blood. The pros win easily because, yes, momentum matters more than effort.

How about every person who has tried to break a bad habit and failed? Momentum matters more than effort.

Look at any area of life and you see that momentum always beats effort. And yet, curiously, it is effort that's commonly lauded and said to be the key to personal development and life. We need minimal effort to do *anything*, of course, but what people don't tell you is that effort has strongly diminishing returns.

Effort has a cost—energy! Thus, no, we don't need "110% effort," because that would leave us with a negative amount of energy soon thereafter. People glorify maximum, all-out effort; it's honored universally, but it's a woeful strategy for creating the greatest returns in life. And this is why:

We can generate momentum with little effort, but great

effort does not always generate an equivalent amount of success or momentum.

I'll give you an embarrassing example of this from my life. For quite a long time, I've had poor self-control, especially with sleep. Unless I absolutely must get out of bed, I find myself unable to force myself to get up early unless I know I have to be somewhere. And yes, I've tried *very* hard.

The one thing, the only thing, that always works for me is finding a way to set my biological clock to the time I want. I can sometimes do it with melatonin. But what always works is staying up later and later until my circadian rhythm naturally resets to a reasonable schedule.

When my sleep schedule eventually cycles through, I can go to bed early and get up at 4 AM naturally. I'll go to the gym for an hour or two and then write at a cafe for a few hours. I'll live a full day before noon!

In my sleep schedule struggles, I've noticed a massive mismatch between effort and results. When my biological clock is set to awaken me at 4 AM, it takes *zero* effort for me to get up, *zero* effort to go to the gym, and *zero* effort to write at the cafe. It's all pleasure. And it's strange, because I've always thought this feat required sacrificial lamb offerings and the combined effort and discipline of 12,058 trained soldiers. In fact, it does require that level of effort *with brute force effort alone.*

* * *

When in a dysfunctional sleep schedule, my effort to sleep and/or get up earlier was extreme, and I still couldn't fix it. I remember lying wide awake in bed for *five hours* one night because I decided to "go to bed early." More effort wasn't the answer; it rarely is.

I say none of this to imply that effort is without value, that effort isn't necessary, or that hard work is futile. I only say this to reiterate the truth: momentum matters more than effort. It does in every case.

You can think of effort as a frisbee in the wind: effort *with momentum* is 50x stronger than effort *against momentum*. If the wind is strong enough, your frisbee may even travel backwards. I've seen it happen! What's most important in this scenario? The frisbee throw (effort) or the wind (momentum)? The wind, of course!

Golden sub-nugget: Stop thinking about trying harder. Lots of people counter-productively overexert themselves already. Don't seek greater effort, seek greater momentum. (The second half of the book is full of specific momentum-generation techniques.)

As a bonus, this perspective is (significantly) more fun than berating yourself for not trying hard enough. You are likely already trying your hardest. It's quite possible that you've tried so hard that you've burned yourself out. Even worse, if your effort didn't generate real momentum, now you have poor results *and* feel exhausted (a sad but common combination for effort purists). As mentioned earlier, the most popular goal structures wear you out and self-destruct. Don't blame yourself, blame the strategies.

Very often, generating momentum is nearly effortless. I understand that may sound too good to be true, but this is actually true. I've proven it, as have hundreds of thousands of others who have read my books.

I've written four books by committing to 50 words a day. Fifty words is one paragraph, the easiest writing assignment ever. Writing a good book is *exceptionally hard work*, which is why I relied on momentum (50+ words every day) more than effort.

Don't get me wrong, I put great effort into writing all of my books! But once you learn how to exert effort *with* the wind, it's not the same. Remember, effort rarely produces a 1:1 result. Try to move a boulder up a mountain. Try to tip a teetering boulder at the top of a mountain. Which one produced a result? These physics concepts are also true in our lives.

I've been writing for 15 years, learning my writing strengths and weaknesses, learning technical aspects of writing, seeing it benefit me and others. I can type fast without looking at the keys (which was not always the case). Do you know how much easier that alone makes everything? I have significant long-term momentum in writing. When I combine that with the short-term momentum generation technique of 50 words a day, I can write a lot of useful books, even though I was born lazy.

I would have never written even one book if I tried to do it with effort alone. And I see this play out in others too. When I tell people what I do, many (most?) of them say they too want to write a book "someday." I love that!

Writing a book is a worthy pursuit and very rewarding. But writing a book requires a gargantuan amount of work, and someone trained us to focus on that difficulty and disregard how momentum can change the situation. Therefore, most people will never write a book, even though surveys say that most people would like to write one!

Golden Nugget: Momentum Makes Effort Feel Different

If you think that a seasoned weightlifter lifting a weight feels the same as a beginner lifting a weight, think again! Let's say that they are each pursuing an identical physical challenge relative to their strength: of 80% of their max weight capability.

Who do you think will fare better? Who will work out

longer? Who will have the better experience? Those are ridiculous questions, right? They're lifting the same weight relative to their strength! But intuition still tells us the newcomer is going to struggle more. Why? Underneath the identical physical challenge is a lopsided mental challenge.

As they feel identical physical resistance...

1. The weightlifter will feel a familiar sense of **satisfaction** and **pleasure** and **progress**.
2. The beginner will feel **annoyed** and even **repulsed** by this alien sensation.

I'm an amateur weightlifter. I do it three days a week. I'm not strong, but I've lifted weights frequently enough over the last several years to change how it feels to lift weights. Over 10 years, how it feels to lift heavy things has changed like this...

Repulsive > annoying > tolerable > kind of satisfying > fun challenge > I grunt with joy

Weightlifting remains the same hard physical work it has always been, but that work feels very different mentally and emotionally now.[2]

Threads of Momentum

Weightlifters have momentum in their muscle memory, in their brains, and in their routines. They are *familiar* with every part of the process and have built up positive associations with each aspect. They even know how good they'll feel after the workout.

The beginner feels the shock of how different weightlifting is than, you know, not lifting heavy stuff. They mentally resist continuing the behavior because it's unfamiliar and takes a lot of mental as well as physical effort. As a beginner, I can remember my brain repeatedly telling me, "Stop. Put the weight down. This sucks. This feels awful. Go eat peanut butter." Today, the only part of that which remains is the peanut butter.

A seasoned weightlifter can (and does) lift for longer, with harder relative weights, and exerts greater total effort than a beginner; not because of their physicality but because of their brain. The body is not our primary limiting factor physically anyway, because that would be dangerous. Do we really want to find out we worked out too hard by seeing our arm fall off?

In most cases, the brain tells the body to stop exercising long before it is dangerous to continue. Thus, the beginner gets the resistance of the weight *and* the full resistance of the brain. Regular weightlifters are not only mentally comfortable with the physical effort required in strength training, they crave it.

When you think about effort, it should always be in the

context of momentum. Of course, Dwayne "The Rock" Johnson outworks almost everyone in the gym. He absolutely puts in more effort if measured in physical exertion or calories burned. But it's not the same effort, is it? His effort exists in a vortex of positive momentum, backed by decades of training, knowledge, and access to premium equipment and nutrition. It's *easier* for him to work out for two hours than for many people to work out for 20 minutes.[3]

Ask Yourself: Will My Effort Be Multiplied or Neutralized?
Imagine two people, Bob and Stan, applying for the same job. They have the same qualifications and experience and will put forth the same effort in the interview. To rule out other biases, let's also say they are identical twins.

Bob is in a state of positive momentum because he has been acting confidently for the entire day. Stan is in a negative state of mind because he has been sulking and worrying all day in bed. Bob will naturally exude more confidence in the interview, which the interviewer will certainly notice.

With two equally qualified candidates, Bob will get the job, and not just because that rhymes. The world is not an empathetic place. More confident people get the jobs. People with short- and long-term positive momentum get "luckier" in life, if you want to call it luck.

The Magic of Momentum

* * *

After the job interview, we will see their momentum compound. Bob, who got the job *because of confidence*, now has one more reason to be confident. Stan missed out on the job *because* of low confidence and now has *less* confidence. Two otherwise identical people are snowballing in opposite directions.

Most people will look to the result of who got the job to explain their situations. They'll say that Bob is lucky because he got the job and that Stan is down on his luck because he didn't. But the job result wasn't the important difference between these two, was it? Remember the frisbee in the wind? It was their preexisting states of momentum that ultimately decided who got the job, and it will continue to decide many other things in their lives until changed.

Think about this example the next time something bad happens in your life. Is it possible that it happened because of your state of mind? Because you let negative emotions snowball today and over time? Nothing is wrong with you if you said yes. **Every person** has missed opportunities or experienced hardship because of negative momentum at some point. It happens because we're imperfect. It's okay, but we need to be aware of it to minimize it.

Terrible things happen to good people all the time, and I know it isn't always their fault. But sometimes—many times—it comes from momentum, which is good, because we can change our momentum instantly. Even if none of a particular problem is your fault, you still need to reverse the negative momentum to improve your situation. Taking responsibility isn't about accepting blame for the past, it's about owning your future.

Care most about momentum, even more than effort, and you will see better results. That means doing more "priming" for momentum and less forceful, shame-driven banging your head against the wall hoping to get somewhere. For example...

- If you want to have a productive day, start by making your bed or cleaning your room for an easy initial win. Use a task system that's organized, easy to use, and encouraging. This produces positive momentum! A simple to-do list can absolutely accomplish this, which is why everyone has heard of them. I use the aforementioned Magnetic Life Management System (MLMS) to start my day with momentum.
- If you want to get a job, focus as much on your sense of self-worth and confidence as your resume, especially on the day of the interview (near-term momentum). There are power poses that can physiologically change your confidence level in two minutes.[4]
- If you want to turn your life around, use a system

like mini habits, which uses easy and small daily habits to build short-term and long-term momentum. Whatever system you use should be momentum accumulative (small actions, easy and stackable wins) instead of degenerative ("big" goals, tempting to skip days).

- If you want to learn piano, make it comfortable, enticing, and easy to play. Don't require yourself to play until your fingers bleed. Let yourself be bad and inexperienced at first without judgment. Easy (forward motion) does it!
- If you want to lose weight, don't go on a crash diet (or any diet). Those require maximum effort for negative results. Instead, use a method that gradually and non-judgmentally changes your relationship with food and never shames you for watching TV or eating dessert. Think small wins that you can stack on top of one another, which can then roll into bigger and bigger wins.

Next, we'll get practical. Until this point, we've discussed the ins and outs of momentum and how it works in our lives. It's time to put all of that knowledge into action.

I get frustrated by nice but forgettable platitudes that never really impact my life. That's why we're going to cover many specific examples and techniques you can use to generate and sustain positive momentum in your life, and also some general and specific ways to reverse negative momentum. Let's go!

Part Two
Mastering Momentum

Manipulation vs Control

The word "manipulation" has negative connotations because of its unfortunate use in relationships. A manipulative person isn't someone you want to spend much time with. That kind of manipulation, however, is only the *third* definition given by Merriam-Webster dictionary.[1] The first two are:

1. to treat or operate with or as if with the hands or by mechanical means, especially in a skillful manner
2. to manage or utilize skillfully

Manipulation is usually good! It's how we create useful things, leverage our skills, and influence results. Your ability to manipulate momentum is essential to your success.

To control something is to have *complete* authority over it. You could say that manipulation is control over *one* aspect of something. As we've all experienced, we can't control every aspect of life. That's okay, or rather, it has to be okay because it's reality. While we can't control everything, we can manipulate important, impactful areas, which will influence the trajectory of our lives.

It's imperative to think about momentum in terms of manipulation instead of control. We can control momentum in broader terms—living in such a way that positive momentum is all but guaranteed. It's hard to predict how much momentum any specific behavior will produce and in what timing; we just know that forward motion will always produce some amount of momentum.

Remember this idea when something doesn't go your way or when your positive momentum is not as strong as you thought it would be after starting an action. Your job isn't to produce a precise amount of momentum, it's to create positive momentum as often as you can. If you do that, results will follow.

Those who try to control every aspect of their lives are more likely to fall apart or spiral downward when setbacks occur. Such people are unprepared to handle the nonstop barrage of imperfections we all experience in life. This effect can worsen further if you read a lot of self-help books, which tell you the "right" ways to think, act, and live. Hyperawareness of the "perfect" way to handle things creates hypersensitivity to failure. Hypersensitivity to failure is demoralizing and may lead to long-term failure, which presents as apathy and self-doubt.

With that said, let's get this straight before we discuss how to master momentum. Not all days will *feel* victorious. Not all small steps forward will produce strong momentum. *Many* will, however, and long-term momentum will bring steadier and more reliable success, which is why consistency is key.

***

Life will throw haymakers at you; you won't block them all. How will you respond then? Listen to what Rocky Balboa has to say about it to his son in the 2006 movie *Rocky Balboa*:

"When things got hard, you started looking for something to blame, like a big shadow. Let me tell you something you already know. The world ain't all sunshine and rainbows. It's a very mean and nasty place and I don't care how tough you are, it will beat you to your knees and keep you there permanently if you let it. You, me, or nobody is gonna hit as hard as life. But it ain't about how hard you hit. It's about how hard you can get hit and keep moving forward. How much you can take and keep moving forward. That's how winning is done!"

Mastering momentum isn't about being unstoppable in every single moment or avoiding all setbacks; it's about being unstoppable in a general sense, as Rocky is saying. It means you can take hits. It means, even if you're knocked out cold, you're going to come to your senses and recover quickly. It means you aren't easily discouraged. It means you know how to move yourself forward in any circumstance.

I could see how someone would read about the magic of momentum and expect every day to be one full of power and success. But that's not realistic, nor is it what this book is about. In fact, it's in those "down" moments that this book will help you the most. The next time you feel defeated, you can remember the magic of momentum and use it confidently, knowing that you will emerge from the other side victorious. Momentum is the way out of bad situations.

Since everyone faces unpleasant situations and negative momentum, we're going to talk about that first. Momentum is easiest to generate when you already have it, but what if you have the wrong kind right now?

Chapter 6
Reversing Negative Momentum

I used to drink soda. Then I stopped. No struggling. No relapses. Since then, over 20 years ago, I've had about one or two sodas per year (if that). I enjoyed soda, but it was never integral to my lifestyle. Once I read about harmful soda ingredients such as high fructose corn syrup and sodium benzoate, it completely transformed how I thought about and understood soda. It was a Jack LaLanne situation.

Jack LaLanne lived to be 96 years old. The day before he died of pneumonia, he reportedly worked out for two hours. At 96 years old. With pneumonia! Jack wasn't always such a workout warrior; he never exercised when he was younger. But one day, he attended a seminar on healthy living and what he learned was an epiphany. From that moment on, he became a workout warrior and one of

America's founding fathers of fitness.

My soda change and Jack's fitness change are not the norm. For example, many people already know about soda's terrible impact on the body or how exercise benefits us, but still struggle to drink less soda and exercise more.

Epiphanies aren't a strategy for change. They are more of a lucky phenomenon that some people get to experience and most others don't. I could do it with soda but not in other areas of my life, which required a different approach, as you'll see. Before we cover that, I'll tell you the brief solution for short-term momentum reversal.

Short-Term Momentum Reversal

The way to reverse (negative) momentum in the short term is as simple as it is when driving a car. If you're going the wrong way, change your direction. **Create positive momentum in a new direction. That's it!**

This solution is comprehensive enough for short-term momentum; specific techniques to change your direction come in the next chapter. The moment you step into a new direction, you've solved any and all short-term momentum problems. Thus, the rest of this chapter will deal with long-term negative momentum, which manifests as frequent and habitual temptation to engage in negative behaviors.

Long-Term Momentum and Brain Maps

Stop smoking. Stop drinking. Stop biting your nails. The phrasing makes it sound like you can simply remove the behavior. But can you?

When you remove something from your life, you need to fill that void with something else.

To be more specific, a behavioral void includes:

Time: When you stop doing X, you must spend that time doing something else!

Emotion: When you remove something that fulfills an emotional need (even if it is an overall negative or bad habit), you must find a new way to deal with that need! Running is counterintuitively a decent substitute for smoking because it provides a "runner's high," which may feel similar to the feeling a person gets while smoking. Smokers often smoke to relax, and running can relax you too.

Brain Map: If you have a bad habit that you want out of your life, only part of your brain feels that way. Another part of your brain sees it as important and integral to your life. If you don't respect that, you will fail to change. But what does this term "brain map" even mean?

Neuroscientists like to talk about brain maps at parties.

Brain maps are essentially the brain's current understanding of life. You have brain maps for your five senses, your habits, your likes and dislikes, and so on. This understanding becomes the basis for behavioral instruction. For example, my brain map associates soda with ideas of good taste, unhealthy, unnecessary, and not worth it. Thus, I rarely drink soda because the negative outweighs the positive. This is different from another person's soda brain map, which may associate soda with these ideas: slightly unhealthy, delicious, feel-good treat, important part of routine. Both brain maps recognize the same pros and cons of soda, but there is a clear difference in the relationship and expected behavior.

Negative areas of our lives (bad habits) have associated brain maps with faulty understanding that gives us faulty instructions. Think about each behavior's brain map taking up a piece of real estate in your brain. **These don't just disappear!** The best way to address a faulty brain map is to redefine it. That means to strategize replacement activities for your bad habit triggers, cravings, and emotional needs. I will get into specific examples soon.

To eliminate a negative behavior, you must think in terms of its brain map and give your brain an alternate understanding of that space. And when I say understanding of that space, I don't mean conscious understanding. Who, while drinking a soda, consciously thinks, "This is an important part of my daily routine and life"? Nobody, I hope, but that's what their brain map could say.

Can you see why so many "just stop doing X" plans fail? If you don't change your brain map, your intention to "stop doing X" only ends up depriving your brain of something it knows and thinks it needs.

The Magic of the Right Replacement

I've had some bad habits, which have varied in intensity and possibly even reached addiction territory. I've noticed that every time I've found a suitable replacement for them that gave me a similar reward, I could phase out the bad habit and increase the substitute. Interestingly, I've noticed that as I moved towards the substitute behavior, very often my desire for *both* behaviors would fade! And this is because of how brain maps work.

I've had the (dis)pleasure of needing to reverse negative momentum in a few areas. I decided to be vulnerable in this chapter about my struggles because I think it will be the most useful for you to see real-world examples from the source. We're going to cover alcohol, gambling, anxiety, and health/fitness.

Negative Momentum Reversal: Alcohol

During the pandemic, I started drinking too much. The

first thing I did is what everyone does. "I'm gonna cut back." It didn't work.

I kept consciously planning to "only have one or two drinks, and not every day." I continued drinking three or more beers per day. What I wanted consciously didn't match my subconscious understanding (brain map) of alcohol. When you look at the brain map below, don't think of these associations as conscious thoughts, but rather subconscious associations based on one's prior behavior and experience.

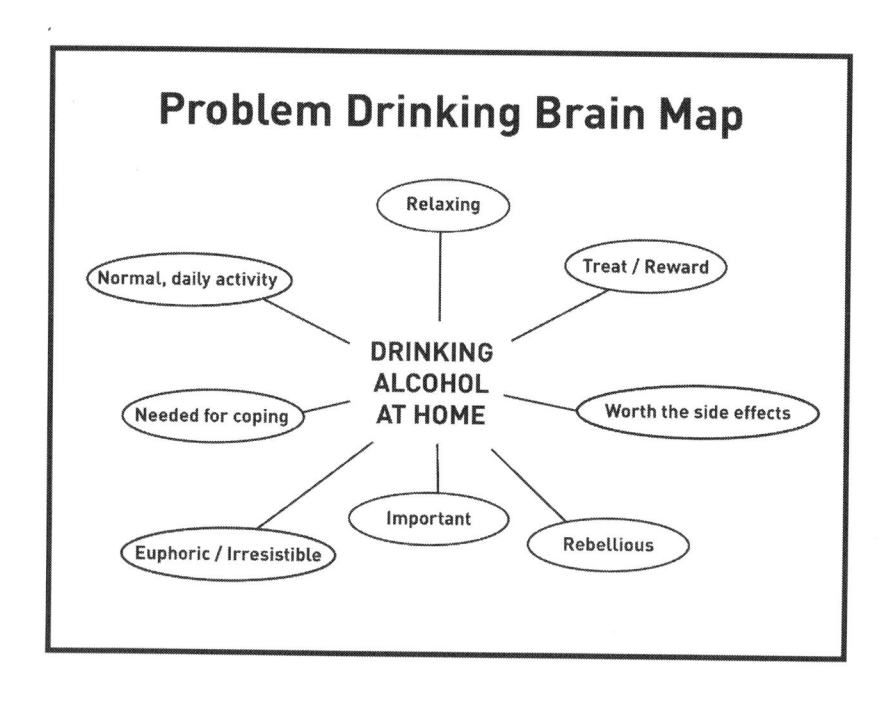

Problem Drinking Brain Map

DRINKING ALCOHOL AT HOME
- Relaxing
- Treat / Reward
- Worth the side effects
- Rebellious
- Important
- Euphoric / Irresistible
- Needed for coping
- Normal, daily activity

I had accidentally trained my brain to develop a dangerous, unhealthy brain map for home drinking. This brain map is exactly why it was normal for me to wonder when I'd "start drinking for the day." It was a given. And it was never one drink. It was usually three to six. I would have 25 to 35 drinks per week, well above the recommended upper level for adult males of 14 drinks per week given by the National Institute on Alcohol Abuse and Alcoholism (NIAAA).

Things changed when I stopped buying real beer and stocked non-alcoholic beer instead. I hypothesized that, aside from the way alcohol made me feel, I mostly drank it to "treat myself." The act itself of "getting a drink" was the primary reward, and the rewarding effects of alcohol were secondary.

In the early days after my switch, I would drink one to three non-alcoholic beers every night. I always drank fewer non-alcoholic beers because they didn't trigger the same pleasure-chasing response that alcohol did. The substitute worked! Today, I don't drink alcohol *or* non-alcoholic beer at home (I'll explain why I don't need the substitute anymore).

Changing a Brain Map: Why My Plan Worked

Problematic behaviors or addictions are most common with experiences or substances that provide *unusually strong brain rewards*. You don't hear about cucumber addictions because, while cucumbers are delicious, the brain reward from cucumber consumption is only moderate, nothing extraordinary. When you experience a euphoric sensation, however, your brain notes it. When you do it repeatedly, it doesn't merely learn to love that behavior, it highlights *that entire area as an important part of your life*. Your brain says, "Wow, this is amazing. Let's see if we can accommodate even more of this stuff." When you think about an addiction or bad habit, the objective is to change how your brain thinks about that area of your life.

Problem drinkers don't need to "cut back on alcohol": they need to change what drinking alcohol means to their brain.

Some people simply want to cut back on alcohol, and can do just that successfully. But they can only do it if alcohol isn't yet elevated to a high level of prominence in the brain (as it is for problem drinkers or alcoholics). It depends on their current brain map. Remember how I said I quit soda easily? Some people can do that with alcohol. Others, like me, need to change their brain map *first*.

Resetting a Euphoric Brain Map

Alcohol brings euphoric feelings because it floods our reward circuits with dopamine. My switch was to non-alcoholic beer (0.5% ABV), which tastes exactly like real beer and also satisfies the urge to treat myself. It looks like beer, tastes like beer, and feels like a treat. The only difference between this experience and real beer was a **lower-intensity brain reward** from drinking.

Three months of fake beers later, my brain map for "home drinking" had changed dramatically.

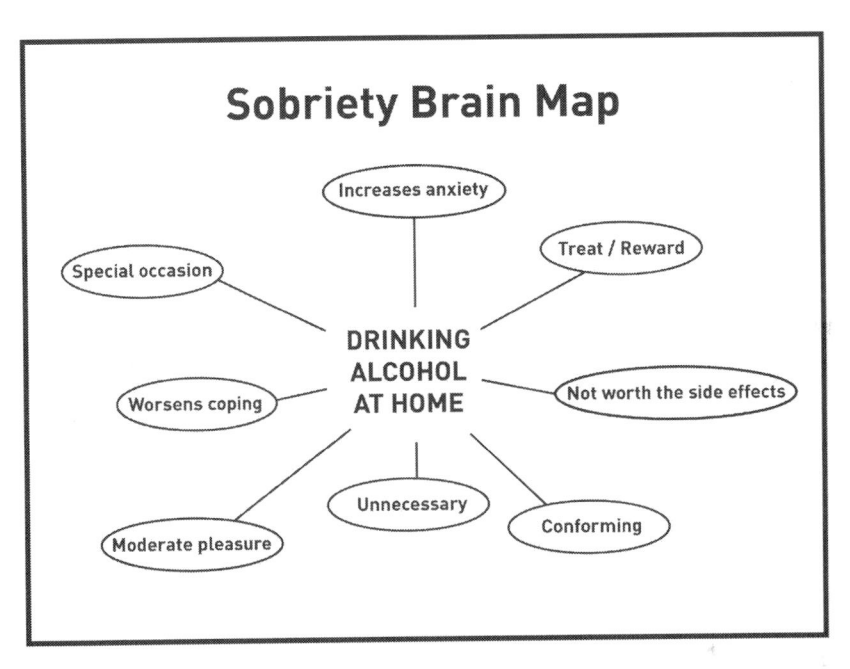

Sobriety Brain Map

- Increases anxiety
- Treat / Reward
- Special occasion
- Not worth the side effects
- Worsens coping
- Conforming
- Unnecessary
- Moderate pleasure

Center: **DRINKING ALCOHOL AT HOME**

You may notice a number of significant changes in this map compared to the last one. In fact, the only area that stayed the same was "Treat/Reward." And yet, the only real change in my behavior was a switch from euphoric reward (6% ABV) to moderate reward (0.5% ABV). To fully understand how this could happen, consider that there is a relationship between the conscious and subconscious mind. Remember how earlier I said that subconscious preferences act like lobbyists? This is a good way to think about it.

* * *

When I switched to non-alcoholic beer that *did not* give me euphoric feelings, my subconscious must have fired its beer lobbyists that kept persuading me to drink. Thus, this change did not only take place subconsciously, but my conscious mind gained significant clarity about alcohol and saw it differently, too. In addition to noticing how I felt better physically and my improved mood, I had less lobbying noise from my subconscious to "just have a drink. Remember how good it feels?" So I was left with memories of dehydration, missing workouts, feeling lousy, and not being as mentally sharp as usual. Without the blinding light of euphoria, I could see all of the less-savory associations.

I don't consider myself to be particularly stout against temptation, but I can resist moderately satisfying things *easily*. It's much harder to resist euphoria. Since this change only applied to inside my home, I continued to drink outside of my home. I would get drunk about once a week at a casino. Interestingly, drinking while out didn't tempt me to drink at home. But then something unexpected happened.

Six months after I gave up home drinking, I stopped drinking outside of my home too. Neurologically, I believe it was my new "home drinking" brain map overtaking my "outside drinking" brain map, which makes sense when you look at the associations. As it stands, I'm a rare/special occasion drinker now. I didn't even try or want to take it this far; my desire to drink simply shrank.

One reason why I like using the syntax of brain maps is that it allows for a more nuanced understanding of behaviors and the brain. For example, I had a different brain map for home drinking and drinking away from home. And then those maps merged into one map. That's incredibly specific and possibly unique to me. This extraordinary flexibility matches everything we know about the brain.

As Norman Doidge says in his superb book *The Brain That Changes Itself*:

"At first many of the scientists didn't dare use the word 'neuroplasticity' in their publications, and their peers belittled them for promoting a fanciful notion. Yet they persisted, slowly overturning the doctrine of the unchanging brain. They showed that children are not always stuck with the mental abilities they are born with; that the damaged brain can often reorganize itself so that when one part fails, another can often substitute; that if brain cells die, they can at times be replaced; that many 'circuits' and even basic reflexes that we think are hardwired are not. One of these scientists even showed that thinking, learning, and acting can turn our genes on or off, thus shaping our brain anatomy and our behavior—surely one of the most extraordinary discoveries of the twentieth century."

***

The brain remapping process:

1. A behavior with powerful reward creates an imbalanced brain map of intense and potentially destructive desire.
2. A substitute behavior is introduced with several similarities to the original behavior, except that the reward is a moderated version of the prior reward.
3. Over time, the brain reclassifies the behavior as something that leads to a moderate reward and thus reverts to a normalized (or less) desire.

This is a game-changing way to think about bad habits. We're not merely abstaining from a behavior to weaken the neural pathways. We're actively reclassifying this brain map as something that *isn't a euphoric experience*. People have already proven this idea to work, in fact, with the drug Disulfiram, which takes this process two steps further.

If you take Disulfiram, drinking alcohol will make you sick. This drug has been around for over 70 years. If it works, to the patient, alcohol goes from so pleasurable that they can't stop themselves from drinking to so unpleasant that they'd rather not drink at all.

While more people should know about drugs like this, it also isn't perfect. For example, some people associate the drug itself, instead of the alcohol, with feeling sick and stop taking the drug. Still, it has worked for many.

Another drug, Naltrexone, lies somewhere between fake beer and Disulfiram. Naltrexone eliminates the pleasurable feeling that you get from drinking alcohol. Again, it's another way to help the brain reclassify the behavior.

- **Non-alcoholic (0.5% ABV) beer:** drinking produces smaller reward
- **Naltrexone or 0% alcohol beer:** drinking produces no reward
- **Disulfiram:** drinking produces pain/sickness (opposite of reward)

"Cutting back" on alcohol does nothing to change the brain map. Your subconscious remains fully aware of the reward of alcohol. You're just depriving it of that reward. For those who haven't trained themselves into a problematic alcohol brain map, this is okay (or maybe their experience isn't as euphoric as it is for problem drinkers and alcoholics). For those who struggle with drinking, they might consider one of the options above to change their brain map.

I think the correct approach depends on the severity of the problem. If, like me, you find yourself liking something a little too much but it's not at a clinical stage, something like non-alcoholic beer could be a great solution. It's going to give you a similar experience but with a more moderate reward.

If you are an alcoholic, it's possible that the more moderate reward of the non-alcoholic beer (0.5% ABV) would only make you crave the real thing even more. In fact, one person told me exactly this when I recounted my experience to him. He very quickly said, "I can't. I'm an alcoholic." In such cases, I would think Disulfiram or Naltrexone would be more suitable. (Note: all serious addictions should be discussed with your doctor. I am not giving medical advice.)

The Crazy Thing that Happened

The most baffling thing about this entire experience is that my desire for non-alcoholic beer *also* vanished. I've had non-alcoholic beer in my fridge for months now and I don't ever drink it. In the beginning of this, I mentioned I would drink one to three of them per day because I craved beer.

It seems that, as my alcohol at home brain map transformed from euphoric to moderate, my non-alcoholic beers became like a lot of other stuff in my fridge. I have pickles in my fridge, and I sometimes go months without having them. I don't need a pickle. Who needs a pickle?

If I get in a pickle mood, I eat a pickle. If I get in a "treat/beer" mood, perhaps when watching a movie, I'll crack open a fake beer and have one or two.

***

As a worldwide bestselling author on habits, my greatest fear for the last decade has been that I would wind up with a crushing addiction. I feel like I've always had an addictive personality and am more susceptible to it than most.

So far, maybe aided by paranoia and obsessive research about the brain, I've been able to keep myself from falling into serious addiction. But I don't know where I'd be now if I had stuck with the "I just need to cut back on drinking" strategy that wasn't working at all. It makes me sad to think of how many others are in that same spot or have given up but don't know about this way of approaching bad habits.

Isn't it fascinating that we can consciously know what Naltrexone is doing or that a beer is actually "fake" with only 0.5% ABV and yet they can still change how our brain classifies alcohol? It happens subconsciously!

Happier

I've been happier not drinking. It's strange because of how much it conflicts with my previous understanding of alcohol. I never understood why they called alcohol a depressant until I stopped drinking it. It also helped to focus on my health and fitness regimens that are so important to me.

***

We often think about tackling bad habits as a sacrifice, as something painful. But that has not been my experience. In each case, my life has improved *and* my cravings for the bad habit have decreased.

When I first received my non-alcoholic beer, I had one real beer left in my fridge. It stayed there for over a month, as I had (in my mind) a better alternative right next to it. I eventually drank it for a special occasion. And now I see water as a better alternative to even the fake beer.

If you mentally absorbed all of that, you can see why brute force willpower to forcibly remove a problematic behavior from your life is most often an ineffective approach to change. When you try to "cut back" on something that your brain loves at a deep, subconscious level, you're going to fail miserably unless you're superhuman. It isn't a smart fight.

Negative Momentum Reversal: Gambling

When I was younger, I went on a cruise with my family to celebrate my grandpa turning 80 years old. I explored the ship and at some point found the casino. With all the games, lights, and sounds, I figured it must be for kids... Right? They kicked me out several times for not being able to grow a full beard yet (I assume), but I continued to sneak back in because it seemed to be the funnest and most interesting place on the ship for kids.

The Magic of Momentum

* * *

Back then, the machines spat out quarters into a tray below the slot machine if you won. I would watch others play and, if I found abandoned quarters, even play some myself! Then the moment came—I put a quarter into a slot machine, pulled the arm, and won $40 in quarters. I furiously herded my winnings into a bucket and ran back to my stateroom. In the top bunk, I counted my quarters repeatedly. I felt rich!

Twenty years later, I've lost a lot more than $40 in quarters in gambling. Whoops. Whether it was that initial experience that planted a seed or a later one that got me interested in gambling, I don't know for sure. I've heard that most gambling addicts are unlucky enough to *win* their first time gambling. The truly lucky ones lose their first time playing, think, "What a waste of time and money," and never go back.

Gambling is expensive and frustrating because the house always wins in the long run, and I can confirm it usually wins in the short run too. Even as short-term entertainment —the only rational reason to gamble—it's flawed, because there are less costly forms of entertainment.

If I'm honest, and I sure try to be, the allure of gambling has been a problem for me in the last few years, or a net negative. It hasn't ruined my life because I've always played within my means, but I'd be better off doing it less.

* * *

Gambling desensitizes the brain in a manner similar to drugs and alcohol. The experience *delights* the brain's reward system. Slot machines are designed for it. After some time, it can make other activities seem boring in comparison and drive riskier betting practices.

Gambling = Expensive Games

At some point, I realized that my love for gambling mostly comes from my love of *games* and *competing*. I love games of all kinds, and gambling is just playing (rigged) games for money. The monetary stakes, lights and sounds, and variability of reward make gambling a very enticing gaming experience for anyone who loves games as much as I do.

RNG (random number generation) makes slot machines work. The moment you press the spin button, the machine generates a set of random numbers that determine your payout, if there is any. Lights, graphics, and sounds are just a fancy "show" for what is a simple calculation that determines your payout for the spin. The fixed payout odds, meanwhile, guarantee the house to make money from players over the long term.

I found a digital card game called Hearthstone that I really enjoy playing, and I've noticed it has similar elements to gambling, notably RNG. Hearthstone has random card generation and other random elements built into the game.

And, like a slot machine, instead of a simple mathematical calculation and display of numbers, it gives the player a show. For example, when your Kaboom bot minion dies, it visibly tosses a bomb that explodes and deals 4 damage to a *random* enemy minion. Such elements make the game visually interesting, and they also have big implications for how well you do in the game. Will your bomb hit a key minion or waste its power on an insignificant minion? It's that unknown that makes RNG elements exciting; this is called variability of reward.

Variability of Reward

If every time you bet a dollar in a slot machine, it paid you back exactly 90 cents (a common slot payback percentage), nobody would play. It would be boring *and* cost you money! But when you vary the reward from nothing to 50 cents to a dollar to hundreds or thousands of dollars, suddenly the game becomes irresistible and makes *billions* of dollars for casinos around the world every year.

Variability of reward gives you the impression that winning at a casino game is possible. And it actually is, in the very short term. The longer you play, the less likely you are to win. If you play a lot, you are mathematically guaranteed to lose.

It's human nature to be drawn to variability of reward, though some, like me, are more drawn to it than others. I can say for certain that it's responsible for a large part of my love for games (most games combine skill, RNG, luck, and variability of reward).

When I started playing Hearthstone, and it engaged me at close to the same level as the casino games but without losing money, I stopped going to the casino as often.

Despite its smaller reward, a good replacement behavior for a bad habit will feel *better* in most ways because it will have a similar-but-less-intense upside and little to no downside.

Not all bad habits or addictions can or will have a suitable 1:1 replacement, and it might take experimentation to succeed. Before I had success with non-alcoholic beer, I tried a few types of aromatic bitters, which had unique and complex flavors like beer. But I didn't like them enough for them to feel like I was treating myself.

Since I usually drank alcohol while gambling at casinos (negative adjacent area momentum), playing Hearthstone at home instead of gambling has resulted in fewer drinks and better health and fitness as a side benefit. After about a month, I stopped drinking at casinos too.

Other things I did:
1. I cancelled my online gambling accounts. We discussed environment earlier, and having access to online gambling is like having a casino in your

house!
2. I self-excluded from a local casino that had enticing slot machines. This means I'm not allowed on their property. If you remove access, it makes success much easier.
3. I play chess now too. I've found I'm very good at losing in chess, just like at the casino. Perfect!
4. I track all gambling wins and losses. Seeing the house edge in hard numbers reminds me of the only role of gambling (entertainment). I have no expectations of winning, which is important to prevent addiction.

By adding alternative games and subtracting opportunities to gamble, my behavior is *very* different today because my "entertainment brain map" has changed (not because I'm a willpower beast). There was a time a few years ago when I would gamble every day online. Now, I gamble 2–4 times a month and bet more responsibly when I do. I also switched to mostly video poker, which has a lower house edge, giving me more entertainment bang for my bucks. That's a significant momentum shift, and my life has been better for it!

Note: I will never claim permanent victory in this or any other potential problem area. For starters, you can always restart a bad habit and are never "safe" from it; a false sense of security is the best way to fall back hard into bad habits. In addition, I don't care to live a perfect life. That sounds stressful and extremely boring.

The real victory with bad habits, as you might guess, is where your brain maps and long-term momentum are. Are you heading in a direction that will make you happy or miserable in the next decade? Do you have things under relative control or are you sliding into darkness? If you have a problem area in your life, what path can you take to change your current brain map?

Negative Momentum Reversal: Anxiety

Relaxation is critical to enjoyment of life, but also performance. Whether you're an athlete or an office worker, relaxation brings greater focus, and greater focus means better execution. A stressed, tense mind can't perform at its best. It's unfortunate but true that anxiety is a very common issue.

I don't have the answer for all types of anxiety; there are many forms and causes of it. I once struggled with a severe bout of general anxiety, and now I want to share a general solution that worked for me and reversed strong negative momentum in this area.

The Time I Forgot How to Relax (and the Power of Indirect Solutions)

There was a time in my life when I didn't know how to relax. I couldn't do it. If I was conscious, I was anxious.

***

Relaxation and anxiety are highly momentum-driven. This may sound strange and unhelpful, but the best way to relax is to already be relaxed. Until an event triggered my anxiety, I had always been calm by default and it came naturally to me.

In a relaxed or semi-relaxed state, you can relax deeper. If you're completely anxious, getting even slightly relaxed is a challenge. It isn't like most things where you can do a little and build on that success. At least, it wasn't for me. At my worst, I would sit in the corner of my bed, visibly shaking without a specific reason. I had a constant feeling of butterflies in my stomach.

I tried so hard to relax, even for a moment. It made things worse, because it drew my attention internally to my anxious state, which only seemed to compound my anxious feelings and worries. What can be less relaxing than trying hard to relax and failing repeatedly? My stress multiplied upon itself!

I tried all the usual stuff. Even breathing exercises made me anxious about the cadence of my breathing. So how did I get out of this mess? How am I calm now?

An Unexpected Reverse in Momentum
Tired of my constant fight to relax, I decided to live with the problem instead of desperately trying to fix it. I

stopped waiting to "get better" to live and resumed one of my favorite playing activities—playing basketball. And, to my surprise, it was only then that I noticed a change and a way out.

"You can't wait until life isn't hard anymore before you decide to be happy."
- Jane Marczewski

Exerting energy through exercise worked in two ways to reverse my anxious momentum.

1. It took my attention off of my anxiety. When you're playing a competitive basketball game, you don't have the luxury to focus on much else.
2. It relaxed me chemically with endorphins and serotonin.

I continued being active and, while it took time to get back to where I was, the relief was instant. The moment you see your momentum shift from negative to positive is thrilling.

At this time, I didn't know that a solution could be *indirect*. I had tried to "fight" my anxiety for months, failing miserably, making it worse. Direct fighting was the only option, I thought, and I didn't want to give up on myself.

Anxiety is a complex issue with different causes. I won't claim this as a universal cure but, in my experience, you can't fight anxiety directly. You can't focus on the sensations you feel as problems to solve. Do *other* things that change your perspective, thought patterns, mind, and body, and let anxiety passively melt away in the background. This goes along with what I said about thoughts, feelings, and actions. Trying to fix your anxious thoughts and feelings is a much worse approach than taking actions.

I wish you could have seen me looking up articles and videos about how to relax. It was a sad sight, but I learned the valuable lesson that not all battles can be won directly.

Sun Tzu says in *The Art of War*, "In all fighting, the direct method may be used for joining battle, but indirect methods will be needed in order to secure victory. In battle, there are not more than two methods of attack—the direct and the indirect; yet these two in combination give rise to an endless series of maneuvers. The direct and the indirect lead on to each other in turn. It is like moving in a circle— you never come to an end. Who can exhaust the possibilities of their combination?"

The direct method is the obvious one. Indirect methods are less obvious but can be more effective for some problems we face. We can and should use both in our lives. For anxiety, I heartily recommend the indirect approach.

There were two other things that greatly helped my mind and body recover from anxiety:

1. Magnesium supplements (magnesium citrate and magnesium oil): magnesium relaxes us at the cellular level!
2. Sensory deprivation tanks: these helped me immensely by teaching me how to relax again. If you haven't heard of this, you float naked in these tanks without sensory input for an hour per session. It's completely dark, with no sound, and the water is close to your body temperature. There's absolutely nothing to stimulate you! In this environment, it's much easier to enter a deep, meditative, relaxed state.

Negative Momentum Reversal: Health and Fitness

The only proper solution to health and fitness is habitual, since your weight is a product of your genetics and habits. By default, your health and fitness behaviors are of the "since childhood" type. You've been moving and eating your whole life.

Eating and movement are almost exclusively habit-driven behaviors. Look at any person and you'll find identifiable patterns in how they obtain food, the types of food they get, and how they eat it. The same goes for exercise.

I struggled to exercise consistently for 10 years until I tried doing one push-up per day (a mini habit). To this day, I'm still riding that wave of long-term momentum. If you find yourself in a state of negative momentum with your weight, your health, or your fitness, the best approach is habit-based. For that, I highly recommend reading my book *Mini Habits for Weight Loss*. I can't adequately cover everything I said there in this broader-focused book, but I will tell you the wonders of the mini upgrade idea from that book.

A mini upgrade is a small improvement to a dietary choice you're about to make. Instead of an intimidating and complete diet overhaul, you can try to achieve a certain number (I recommend three) of mini upgrades every day. Maybe start with one, then add in more as you get comfortable.

The mini upgrade works seamlessly with your current lifestyle and dietary patterns. Say you're at a restaurant you frequent. Ask yourself, "What's one thing I could do to make this meal slightly healthier than usual?" It may be drinking water instead of soda or getting a side salad instead of french fries. Perhaps it's only eating to 80% fullness and not trying to "clean your plate." Not only do these upgrades add up meaningfully, but by getting into the habit of doing this, you will also learn to "lean" healthy, which is the crux of healthy living.

Think about this from a brain map perspective. If you get into the habit of making healthy upgrades in your dietary choices, it will become a normal part of your dining experience. Over time, this can compound, because we gain affinity for familiar tastes and choice patterns. To the people who hate vegetables, the most likely explanation is that they never eat vegetables.

Processed food addicts face a similar situation to mine with alcohol. Healthy food is like non-alcoholic beer. It provides a smaller brain reward, but you can make it to taste great and it can provide you with what you want and need (micro and macronutrients). It is rewarding, but not as euphoric as processed food.

Too many people force raw kale down their throats and cut out all pleasure associated with eating. They punish their bodies with brutal workouts right away. This is like when I decided to stop drinking alcohol at home without a substitute, cold turkey. It didn't work because I made myself choose between euphoria and deprivation. I don't know about you, but I prefer euphoria. Don't make that the decision.

In habit-driven areas like health and fitness, slow, small, steady changes are always going to work best.

Negative Momentum Conclusion

Whatever the form of negative momentum you are currently dealing with, there are solutions out there. To find them, you need to understand the root cause of your relationship with the behavior causing you problems. You need to think about your brain map in that area. Then you can come up with a targeted plan to supplant that behavior with a healthier one and change the way your brain sees that area of your life. That will begin your transformation from negative momentum to positive momentum.

Regardless of your exact path, at some point sooner rather than later, with smart strategy and a bit of effort, you can turn negative momentum into a small amount of positive momentum, which can compound into life-changing momentum. Let's discuss how to do that.

Chapter 7
Creating Positive Momentum Now (Short-Term Solutions)

This chapter is about short-term momentum, but, to introduce it, I need to explain why short-term positive momentum is the glue that holds *everything* together.

Long-term positive momentum is the ultimate prize because it works passively for you. It's a completely different game when your brain learns to crave the difficult-but-rewarding behaviors that make for a good life. That's why I've written my previous four books about habits.

Here's the odd thing: to get the coveted long-term momentum, you must first be able to generate short-term momentum consistently. Any goal, even one that fails after two weeks, is driven by short-term momentum for as long as it lasts. It's just that most people don't do it consistently enough to get exponential results.

Double a penny every day, and you will have over $5,000,000 in 30 days. But what if you stopped after 14 days? That will net you about $164. That's the difference between consistency and sporadic effort.

To get dreamlike results, you must show up every day! That requires **commitment**.

The logic flows like this:

1. Long-term momentum requires **consistent** short-term momentum.
2. Short-term momentum requires a **commitment** for consistency.
3. What does commitment require for success?

The Key to Commitment

When someone asks me for a favor, I never say yes until I hear it. I will simply ask, "What is it?" Otherwise, this could happen.

Person: "Can you do me a favor?"
Me: "Of course." (Commitment made)
Person: "Give me a million dollars and your gallbladder."
Me: "Uh... Sorry. I can't do that favor." (Commitment

broken)

That's a silly example, but the concept is valid. The higher the ask, the less likely we are to commit to it (even if we previously promised ourselves or others). Commitments are much easier to keep when they ask *less* of you.

You can consistently create short-term momentum with small commitments.

Certainly, this is a nod to my previous books, such as *Mini Habits*. But there are numerous opportunities to generate short-term momentum outside the realm of habit. Sometimes, we need to move forward despite not feeling up to it, not having a habitual base, and not being in the ideal context for action. For those times, you can use the following techniques to help you aim small and keep winning.

The Power of Leaning and the Tipping Point

The moment you push a boulder resting atop a hill is anti-climactic. The push isn't amazing, and the boulder only moves a little. If you were to judge the action and result instantly, you might be disappointed. In the moments that follow that first moment, however, the boulder gains astonishing momentum.

* * *

This is the tipping point, the point at which momentum becomes nearly unstoppable. It's a wild ride for what starts out as something barely noticeable.

"Sure, Why Not?"

Mayonnaise, with soybean oil as the typical main ingredient, is one of the worst foods for your waistline.

The average British person will eat 18,304 sandwiches in their lifetime.[1] A serving of mayo (2 tsp) is 90 calories. Over a lifetime, the difference between someone who adds mayonnaise to their 18,304 sandwiches and someone who skips the mayo is more than 1.6 million soybean-oil-dominated calories. I always get mustard without mayo, and, for the same serving size of 2 tsp, mustard is only six calories.

At my local grocery store's deli one day, a man behind me ordered a sub. The deli employee asked him if he wanted mayonnaise, to which he replied, "Sure, why not?"

His phrasing really caught my attention because, when I get a sandwich, I decline mayonnaise in the same nonchalant manner that this man accepted it. I enjoy the taste of mayonnaise, but I don't *need* it to enjoy a sandwich and I know that soybean oil is horrible, so I think, "Meh, I can skip it." Over a lifetime of delicious sandwiches, these slight leans make a massive difference... a lifetime difference of 1.6 million calories of mostly soybean oil!

***

Added to that, every time you make a choice like this, you set a precedent for the next time. When this man orders a salad, will he choose the healthier oil and vinegar or the tastier ranch dressing? If I had to guess, I think he'd say, "Why not ranch?" Such small leans are everything in life.

The Supreme Importance of Leaning

How do you feel about walking one lap around the block? Or doing one push-up? Neither is an intense exercise. You wouldn't say, "Wow, she's really getting after it!" These behaviors are not too far removed from sitting on the couch, but they're *juuust* on the exercise side of the fence.

As anyone who has sat on a fence before knows, a slight lean to one side of it is a big decision indeed! When you are on a fence, proverbial or not, even a subtle lean activates the tipping point, and subsequent motion is *highly likely* to be substantial and on that same side of the fence.

- An exercise mini habit can tip you into excellent fitness.
- Smoking a cigarette one time can tip you into addiction and premature death.
- Writing that first word of the novel you've always wanted to write can tip into a completed novel later.
- Saying hello can tip you into a lifelong marriage. It's happened many times!

***

The tipping point, as crucial as it is, never feels that way. It never looks that way. It's a nonchalant "Why not?" It's only the very beginning of the process, and it simply can't yet confer the magnitude of the momentum to come.

Instead of making grand plans and sweeping changes, look for opportunities to *lean* into your desired lifestyle. The results will amaze you.

In time, you'll see that a small lean most often means a bigger, more productive leap. This is the base mindset of a successful short-term momentum generator. They look for ways to lean forward. Now let's look at more advanced techniques and perspectives.

Mindset Strategies

The way you think about and approach action determines how often you act and how focused you'll be as you do. This section will give you a few pieces of mindset advice that can make a big difference in your ability to move forward in a variety of circumstances.

Mindset: Be a Persistent Starter

Abandoned goals and unfulfilled dreams are the painful consequences of being a poor finisher, right? Poor finishers move from one idea to the next, never reaching significant success in any of them. But what if I told you that their problem isn't that they are "poor finishers?"

***

If you aren't following, let's say you start a goal and you quit before you reach your target. What precisely went wrong? Most would say that you quit or didn't finish. Of course, that's what happened, but *why* didn't you finish? What was the actual *mechanism* that caused your failure to finish?

You stopped starting. On one day or in one moment, *you chose not to start again*. That's why you didn't finish. A failure to finish is unequivocally a failure to start again.

It's more helpful to focus on being a continuous starter because starting is actionable and it always results in finishing, so long as you start as much as necessary until the job is done. The timing will vary, as will your "traction" in any individual session of work, but if you want to be the person who never gives up and always finishes, commit to being the most persistent starter.

We sometimes get hung up on the heaviness and pressure of finishing a big project. But, when broken down into real world action, it's merely a large number of decisions to start. Don't let the weight of finishing distract you from the easier and more effective decision to start.

Mindset: Be Playful and Experimental rather than Serious and Intense

There's constant pressure on us to live in the right way,

whether it's coming from ourselves, parents, spouses, family members, religion, books, or authority figures. A fully aware individual might feel it all. And what does that produce?

Stiff. Calculated. Measured. Overanalyzed. Movements.

Paralysis, essentially.

The more pressure we feel, the more we worry about and overanalyze our approach. That's not good because momentum doesn't happen until there's *motion*. When you know something will benefit you, it's almost always best to start moving toward it soon as possible, before you have everything figured out and before it feels comfortable. To make that easier, reduce the pressure you feel.

Here's something you can try right now or later today. There's likely something you want to do more of, but resist. These mysterious mental blocks are often the result of pressure to do things "right," i.e., perfectly.

Suggested action: Whatever your desired activity, dismiss any idea of the "right" way to go about it, the "right time" to do it, the minimum acceptable amount of it, and other such prerequisites. Think this instead: "Forward motion is good, even if it is messy, feels off, and isn't the best timing. Even if I fail, I will learn from it." Then go! Move ahead and embrace the uncertainty.

***

Yes, this is poor advice for something like walking a tightrope with no harness. But 99.59224% of life's ventures are not lethal.

This practice will be especially effective for any areas of your life with baggage. In trying to be the best people we can be, we can pick up some awful feelings associated with doing that.

- Shame: about your work ethic, your prior choices, your fitness level, your excuses, your tarnished reputation, or your lack of success.
- Doubt: about your ability, about your worth, about your choices, about how you spend your time, about the result of considered actions.
- Anger and frustration: about how far you have to go, about the process, about the difficulty, about results you can't control, about deserving more in life than you've gotten.

Sheesh. Those are some *heavy bags*. Letting go of heavy expectations will feel wrong at first. For example, my writing (including this book) is fraught with pressure. There's the pressure of making each book my best one, because anything else feels like regression and that's scary. There's the pressure of knowing I'm an imperfect writer. Every author who releases a book does so knowing that it could be better. You could spend a lifetime writing one book and hopefully it'd be good, but it still wouldn't be perfect.

I am familiar with several flaws in the way I write books. I cannot fix them all and, in trying to fix some, I may create additional problems. Woe to me, because I have to continue writing with that knowledge. It's no wonder that writer's block is a thing, and it's exceptionally easy to *not write anything*. To let go of that baggage feels wrong because it's genuinely important. I care about the value I provide in my books.

But, while it may feel wrong to let go of baggage, here's why it's right: we can't be at our best when encumbered.

When I let go of that pressure and approach my writing with lighthearted curiosity, playfulness, and intrigue, not only do I stop resisting work but I also *enjoy it and produce better content*. As a writer, the best you can hope for is to write something that you are personally proud of. Anything else is too dangerous. The saying is true—you can't please everyone.

I think sometimes about the filmmaker M. Night Shyamalan. He's the *Nickelback* of filmmakers—he gets a lot of bandwagon hate.

"M. Night should be banned from ever making movies again."

"M. Night Shyamalan, please stop."

"M. Night Shyamalamadingdong strikes again."

These are just some of the comments you can find online about M. Night Shyamalan. People absolutely *love* to say he hasn't made a good film since *The Sixth Sense*. And yet, M. Night Shyamalan continues to make films. As he should.

If Shyamalan absorbed and focused on all of the negative opinions about his work, he might stop. That would be a shame, because I would rather see one of his unique-but-flawed films than *Fast and Furious 39*.

Drop the pressure to please everyone and you will please more people because of the mental freedom you gain to do your best work. Choose to be okay with disappointing some people if it means you can live the life you want.

Mindset: Stop Overvaluing Milestones

Does it annoy anyone else that so many things are arbitrary? Why is it so significant to become a millionaire? It's only marginally better than $985,000 and yet we treat it like it's a completely different amount of money.

Why do we celebrate completed marathons of 26.2 miles, but not 20-mile runs? Who decided that turning 50 was more monumental than turning 47? What exactly is wrong with a 23-minute workout? The world is obsessed with clean, arbitrary numbers, but they are no more significant than the surrounding ones. I mean, one million and one dollars is objectively better and more significant than one million dollars, but nobody cares about that extra dollar unless it's the one that takes you to seven digits.

I understand clean numbers give simple, memorable, and familiar reference points. And, no, I don't set meetings at 2:49 PM just to prove a point. But when we apply this concept across a dynamic life, we may only improve 50% when we could have improved 69% simply by being open to fractionated progress.

Instead of joining the world in valuing arbitrary milestones, it's better to value all amounts of progress. An example: I have a pull-up bar in an open doorway in my home. I will randomly do pull-ups when I pass by. That's not a workout. It's not a milestone. But it's a micro dose of exercise, and that's a lot better than nothing! A small 2022 study found strength increases of 10% when participants did only three seconds of strength training per day for a month.[2] *Three seconds.*

When you value progress over milestones and clean numbers, you'll stop getting stuck and discouraged as often in your journey. It's fine to have something concrete to aim for, but it's not okay if that milestone makes you devalue the journey and smaller amounts of progress you make *before* you get to that magic number.

***

The Kitchen Timer Conquers Overwhelm

The standard kitchen timer is one of the greatest productivity inventions of all time. Not a timer app on your phone. Not a digital timer. A standard 60-minute twist timer. I'm using one as I write this, because it annihilates feelings of overwhelm.

Overwhelm is the feeling of having too much to handle at once. It is one of life's greatest hindrances to action. Wouldn't you agree? And yet a $10 kitchen timer can solve it.

A Beginning and End

By twisting my timer to the right and setting it to, say, 25 minutes (this session), I have given myself a clear start time (now) and end time (in 25 minutes). Most of the time, this is all I need for a great, focused session that often exceeds my original aim. But sometimes cats happen.

In this current writing session, my kittens have *repeatedly* distracted me for playtime. I have little interest in fighting said catstractions, as it is one of life's great pleasures.

Distractions are commonplace in today's technology- and cat-driven world. The twist timer, however, takes them in stride. After cat time, I can estimate how much I've "cheated" my work timer and add those minutes back on the timer with a short clockwise wrist twist. It's adaptive conveniences like this that make the twist timer great. But I haven't yet explained its core benefit—boundaries.

Think about this: by creating time boundaries for an activity, you shrink its size from *infinite* to *finite*. Gadzooks!

There is an infinite amount of work you can do right now. How many words do I need to write in order to be "finished" with writing for today... or my life? There's no limit! And writing is one of infinite areas I can pursue. Infinite work in infinite areas is infinitely overwhelming!

Imagine that these infinite tasks are beasts (because analogies are fun?). Using a twist timer is like getting out a virtual lasso and taming one of the infinite task-beasts. Not only does a timer constrain the time you'll give to a behavior, it also *isolates* the behavior from other behaviors so you can focus on it.

If your overwhelm were literally manifest as a pen full of wild animals that you needed to tame, what would your first step be? Assuming you will not use chemical warfare on the poor creatures, the solution is to lasso them one by one. You will not restrain three wild goats and a crazy chicken at the same time.

A kitchen timer works well for this because of its intuitive use, speed, and flexibility. Digital timers are okay, but they require pressing several buttons in a particular order and aren't as easy to add or subtract time on the fly. While this may seem inconsequential, subtle differences like this can be the difference between success and failure.

Here's how to conquer overwhelm with a kitchen timer:

Choose your target. You can only do one thing (well) at a time. Which one of your wild task-animals are you going to tame right now? The other tasks aren't going anywhere. Don't worry about picking the best one (perfectionism); pick a good one. *You will never regret working on a worthwhile task, even if it isn't the technically perfect choice for the moment.*

Make the task finite. How much time do you want to dedicate to this beast of a task? You can do it the way a thief picks a lock. *Feel* your internal reaction to different times.

45 minutes? Cringe. I feel way too tired for that and I have a meeting soon.
30 minutes? A little scary.
17.58 minutes? I can do that!

Chances are, one will feel right and "click." It will be the time that carries little resistance but offers a meaningful reward or sense of progress. If you're not sure, just go smaller than you think. It's much better to work extra time than to fall short or not start because you have selected too much time.

Twist and go. Turn the timer and get to work. With this final move, your overwhelm should shrink because your infinite zoo of infinite task-beasts is now a single, finite, lassoed task-beast you can focus on. If you prefer, you can write your task on an actual cow and rope that dairy queen in real life. Do it for the symbolism!

When your timer runs out, repeat this process as needed. You can continue on the same task or choose a new one. Sometimes, you won't even need the timer anymore if you get into a rhythm of focus.

Bargaining

We've covered how to get your mind in the right place for action.

- Commit to being a persistent starter and trust that as long as you keep starting, you'll finish.
- Be more playful and experimental in your approach than serious and pressure-driven. Accept nine minutes of yoga.
- Conquer overwhelm with a kitchen timer. It will sharpen your focus and give you clear boundaries and expectations (instead of *infinite work*).

***

Those are fundamental ways to live an action-first lifestyle. If you still aren't there yet, it's time to pull out the big guns. Bribery.

Bribery has worked for thousands of years, so we might as well use it on ourselves, which is… *checks laws*… legal! There are two ways to bargain (or bribe) your way into action and momentum.

Reward Bargaining (Bribery)

Reward bargaining uses an incentive to provoke action. You are both the buyer and the seller. As the seller, you are a mercenary offering your services. The bathroom needs cleaning, but you're a mercenary and you don't work for free! Set your price at something the buyer (also you) will pay for work.

If I clean the bathroom, I'll get this reward: _____

It's that simple. It's also very effective. I can't tell you how many times I've used a trip to the theater or a guilt-free video game session to inspire a fantastic work session.

Too many people treat themselves as slaves, making themselves work for "free." That kind of self-relationship makes you resent the boss (you)! Instead, occasionally offer yourself incentives for meeting intraday challenges. Try to make the reward match the effort, too. Giving yourself a new car for cleaning your desk seems a little imbalanced. A piece of candy for 10 hours of garage work in the heat also seems a little off. Find the balance that satisfies.

Ego Bargaining (No Reward)

The ego can be a fantastic provoker of action. What amazes me is that the classic elementary school "Chicken! Chicken!" taunt still works in adulthood. There's something about a challenge to the ego that makes us say, "What?! You dare challenge *me* with *that*?! *Of course* I can do that!"

When I feel lazy, I can often turn my mindset around by taunting myself.

"Stephen… are you scared to exercise? Are you unable to handle it? Are you choosing to be weak?"

Goes to gym

I don't always talk to myself that way, but it can work occasionally if you need to snap out of a mental funk.

Ego bargaining is most effective in areas you take pride in. For example, I've always seen myself as an athlete, I'm competitive, and I take pride in being good at sports or physical challenges, so any sort of physical challenge riles me up to compete. If you take pride in your creativity, you can challenge yourself to create something that only you could create. If you take pride in your green thumb, challenge yourself to take your garden to the next level.

With these two types of bargaining, you can get yourself moving, even when motivation, willpower, and energy are low. For times when you feel paralyzed from emotional turmoil, consider using a seven-second spark.

Seven-Second Sparks (Emotion Regulation)

Sometimes, we may feel as if our emotional state presents an unscalable wall between us and our desired destination. Fear not, because you can break through that wall in seven seconds!

Starting is the hardest part, but why? It's because of inertia, which is "a property of matter by which it continues in its existing state of rest or uniform motion in a straight line, unless that state is changed by an external force." It's another way of stating the first principle of momentum—*you're most likely to do what you just did.* Starting something new requires **force** to break through the inertia of your current state but, once you do, inertia helps you!

Action is magical because it changes your state of being. In mere *seconds*, you can go from feeling depressed to feeling alive—working out, making music, or diving into an exciting project. Thus, to make it easier to capture this magical change, we are going to use a technique to break through inaction and its associated inertia. Seven-second sparks.[3]

Seven-second sparks remove the formality, weight, and overanalysis of a considered action.

Earlier in this chapter, we talked about taking a more playful and experimental approach to action. These are concrete, specific ways to do that.

While "spark" is the key word used, these can actually serve a lot of different purposes. They can relieve you, encourage you, ground you, excite you, and, of course, spark you to further action. Some may scoff at these for their simplicity and duration, but don't scoff too hard until you try them!

Not all of these will be time-based, but they will all include the word "seven" for simplicity. There's nothing scientifically special about seven seconds. It is extremely important, however, to have something *specific* and *memorable* to recall when you need it. "Seven-Second Spark" has the alliteration and flow that makes our hearts sing. Here we go.

Improve Your Feelings with Action (Seven-Second Sparks)

The following seven-second sparks can target and improve emotional issues that leave you feeling stuck. Remind yourself just how *easy* it is to do any of these. The following sparks can help you shift yourself into a better place (and headspace).

Seven slow, deep breaths
Use for: anger, fear, anxiety, overwhelm, stress, temptation

To maximize the impact of these breaths, you can do them meditatively. Try it now just to see how different you feel afterwards. Close your eyes if you wish and focus all of your attention on the simple mechanism of breathing in and out, and do it slowly seven times. I like to pay attention to my jaw muscles loosening up with each exhale, as that seems to reinforce my relaxation (realizing that you're relaxing relaxes you!).

It's easy to breathe, which contrasts beautifully against the stresses and complexities of a modern life.

Slow, controlled, deep breathing is effective because it relaxes us physiologically. This means you don't have to worry about "performance," as relaxation will happen at a biological level. If done meditatively, it can also relax an anxious mind.

Tip: Back when I first tried deep breathing, I'd breathe in deeply, and then exhale quickly and breathe in deeply again. It was not very relaxing. Don't just breathe in slowly, also breathe out slowly, and even pause for a moment before you inhale again. This is how you can ensure physiological relaxation. If you rush any of the three phases (in, out, brief pause), you may not feel much of a difference.

There are also different cadences you can try, in terms of breathing in for X seconds and breathing out for X seconds. There is some science and literature out there on the "best" timing. But I don't want to complicate what should be simple and easy.

If you focus too much on perfecting your deep breathing, it won't be as relaxing. Breathe slowly and deeply in a way that feels natural, comforting, and unforced.

Seven push-ups (substitute with easier knee or wall push-ups if needed, or pull-ups if desired)
Use for: lethargy, anger, anxiety, discouragement, stress, depression, overwhelm

The humble push-up is powerful. It is a functional bodyweight exercise. You can do push-ups anywhere (I recommend elevators). The power of this spark is multifold.

- Blood flow: Push-ups, like all exercises, increase blood flow in your entire body. This can give you a jolt of energy and bolster your creativity (thanks to increased blood flow in the brain). Creativity is an

underrated life skill, as it doesn't merely apply to work projects. Your creativity can help you solve everyday problems, including how you deal with negative emotions.
- New narrative: If you previously felt lazy or "down," doing push-ups presents concrete real-time evidence that contradicts that idea. It tells a new story of an active fighter. That's better.
- Energy outlet: Exercise invigorates the body—we already talked about blood flow—but it also releases calming endorphins and burns off anxious energy. That makes the humble push-up an overall stabilizing activity, as it relaxes us *and* gives us energy!

Seven seconds to call someone
Use for: any emotion

If you have a best friend or family member who is always there for you, count yourself lucky. For all the techniques we have for dealing with emotions ourselves, sometimes it's the empathy, wisdom, and understanding of a friend that can help us the most. And, with technology, we can often reach people in merely seven seconds!

Most people are happy to help and be there for those they care about. It feels good to be a good friend, so unless you're calling someone to complain often, don't feel you're being a burden. Call them with confidence and tell them you'll be there for them as well. And, if in doubt, ask them if you can vent to them. They'll let you know.

Seven seconds to leave the room/situation
Use for: anger, depression, apathy

Sometimes, you simply need to move. Maybe you're in an argument and know you're going to say something you regret. Tell the person you need to cool down and leave the room.

There are other times when you feel stuck, perhaps creatively; in those cases, it can be very useful to leave your current environment. Leaving your current environment is powerfully symbolic for leaving your current (negative/stuck/bad) mental situation. You can change a situation quickly with decisive action!

Seven seconds to power pose
Use for: low self-esteem, self-doubt, fear, worry

We are highly influenceable creatures. Even our body language affects our brain chemistry. A power pose is simply a body position that is associated with being powerful. Think of any athlete who wins a big competition. Their hands go up every time for the victory pose. Winning makes us feel powerful and, when we feel powerful, we take up more space as a sign of dominance.

* * *

A well-known experiment by Amy Cuddy found power poses could change us at the chemical level.[4] This is interesting, because we already knew that confident, powerful people posed their bodies accordingly (such as a winning athlete). But what we didn't know is that acting as if you are powerful, regardless of how you feel, can affect how you feel. It's apparently a two-way street. "Fake it 'til you make it" is a valid strategy!

If you think about it, it makes sense, doesn't it? There are very few aspects of human life that are unidirectional. As covered earlier, there's the relationship between thoughts, feelings, and actions. All affect all, and Cuddy's study shows that.

Winners **feel** victorious and **act** victorious by putting their arms in the air.
People can **act** victorious by putting their arms in the air, and then **feel** more like winners.
(It's also reasonable to assume that people who **think** they are winners are likely to **feel** and **act** that way as well.)

In the study, people assumed either a high- or low-power pose and held it for two minutes. Incredibly, that short amount of time was enough to change their cortisol and testosterone levels.

High-power pose results
20% testosterone increase (confidence and aggression UP)

25% cortisol decrease (stress DOWN)

Low-power pose results
10% testosterone decrease (confidence and aggression DOWN)
15% cortisol increase (stress UP)

The high-power posers became more confident as the low-power posers became less confident and more stress-reactive. What an astonishing change for just two minutes of action!

You may think, "You're saying seven seconds when this experiment was for two minutes. Fool of a Took!" That's why these are called seven-second *sparks*. Do the power pose for seven seconds and see where it takes you. This is a great technique to try, especially prior to big performances or events, such as shows, dates, or interviews. And, of course, if you want to do a full two minutes of power posing, do it. But if you resist it, try seven seconds first.

Drink seven ounces of water
Use for: lethargy, dehydration

If you think dehydration isn't an emotion, try getting dehydrated. Actually... don't! Dehydration is awful and dangerous. Water is excellent for staying energetic, alert, and focused. If you feel off physically or have low energy, drinking water is a good first step.

***

Make sure you measure out exactly seven ounces. <— That is a joke.

Easy, Yet Powerful

These seven-second sparks are beyond easy to do. They cut through intimidation, fear, and doubt with ease. And, despite the low effort they require, they can facilitate instant change. The next time you find yourself in a tough spot, remember that you have an arsenal of seven-second sparks to change the dynamic of your situation!

And these ideas only scratch the surface. Create your own seven-second sparks and add them to your war chest, ready to use any time you need short-term momentum! It will astonish you what a seven-second commitment can do to improve your mood and outlook for the day.

It's more important to remember this concept than it is to remember the specific sparks. This concept makes forward motion much easier than it usually seems to us.

Chapter 8

Sustaining Positive Momentum for Life (Long-Term Solutions)

So, you're in a place of positive momentum. Great! How do you stay there for good?

There are no guarantees in life, as we can't predict the type or severity of obstacles we'll face. We can, however, establish practices that generate momentum in a variety of circumstances.

Create Momentum-Generating intentions

The longer momentum lasts, the more powerful it becomes. Human momentum happens in the short term and long term. If you have done something long enough to create long-term momentum and you are still generating short-term momentum, you are effectively a juggernaut of momentum. Unstoppable!

Sustainability is critical. Anyone can generate momentum on a good day. It's the days that test us, the days we feel off, the days we feel discouraged that decide the sustainability of our momentum generation. For your momentum to survive, you must get your intentions straight.

Why Intentions Are about Commitment
Intention does not produce a 1:1 action result. Every abandoned goal speaks to that. We don't do everything we intend to do. We may do more than we intend to do.

There is value in precise intention, but context is key. For example, planning to start your garden on Wednesday by buying seeds at 2 PM and planting them at 2:30 PM is more likely to succeed than planning to start your garden "sometime" or even "tomorrow." Specificity and precision in intention are a double-edged sword in the same way that marriage is—the commitment tells you exactly what's expected, and fulfilling it can create lifelong happiness. But, if it's broken for any reason, you'd be better off having not made it.

Divorce rates are very high, especially considering how unpleasant a thing it is. A commonly cited reason for divorce is that the couple "grows apart." Two people who used to have a lot in common maybe changed significantly as they aged and not in the same way as their partner. I know for one that I'm a completely different person at 36 than I was at 20, and many people get married in their 20s.

Broadly speaking, people divorce because they no longer find their spouse suitable for them. In the same way, when we set a goal, our circumstances can change later to make our original commitment seem unsuitable.

Life is unpredictable and people change, which makes long-term commitments difficult (whether to people or pursuits/goals).

The solution to this may seem complicated, but it's actually straightforward, staring us in the face. If specific intentions are powerful and preferable to nonspecific intentions (which are more easily ignored) but they are also susceptible to future uncertainty and change, **we need to be specific in the short term and flexible about the methods we use for long-term plans**. I'll give you an example from the business world.

Chipotle is my favorite place to eat and I eat there several times a week. When the COVID-19 crisis hit, it was a challenge for their business. People weren't going out to eat. Not only did this lower dine-in sales, but it also put major question-marks over their expansion plans.

* * *

As one of their most loyal customers, I saw firsthand how Chipotle reacted, and it was impressive. They streamlined their online takeout and delivery systems, to the point of having specific chefs and kitchen staff for online orders at some locations. They also focused on their delivery app, which is now the easiest and best I've ever used for food delivery.

Instead of carrying on with their original plan to open new standard restaurants, they are now opening some restaurants that accept only online orders and don't have a dine-in area. This benefits them (lower footprint and overhead costs) and their customers (faster service). Not only did this suit the social distancing world, but it also meshed with the rising long-term trend of food delivery.

Chipotle's long-term plans to grow and improve their business have remained intact. Their ability to pivot and react to unforeseen circumstances has resulted in even better results than their initial plans, especially since many of their competitors have not done the same. Chipotle's online orders *tripled* in the 3rd quarter of 2020; their flexibility has a lot to do with their stock price soaring since the pandemic hit in March 2020.

This is *exactly* how we should operate in our own lives. We can have ambitious plans, but we can't bank on them to play out *exactly* as we'd think. The intentions we live out today should be fresh and based on current conditions. A year from now, we might live on Mars, for all we know! We should set precise intentions, but not for next month; let's set them for today or, better yet, for *this moment*.

The fresher your intention is, the more likely it is to come true.

Think about that boldface sentence. If you intend to do something *this instant*, you're deciding based on *current* information. People don't divorce 10 minutes after they get married. It happens later, when the situation has changed in a way they didn't expect.

Intentions that consistently generate momentum have these three qualities:

1. They align with a longer-term goal or ideal (strategy).
2. They are based on *current* information (tactics).
3. They are doable (ability).

If we omit any of these, we lose momentum. Here is an example of each.

No Strategy = No Direction + No Momentum

Day 1: Alex walks to the pond today. Why? She doesn't know.
Day 2: Alex writes poetry. Why? Your guess is as good as hers.

Day 3: Alex sleeps in until 1 PM, then goes camping for no reason.

What has Alex accomplished? Where is her momentum? It's hard to say, because nobody knows what she's doing, including her. Her life seems interesting, but it lacks clear direction. I suppose that's okay if she's enjoying herself, but most of us have aspirations, and I'm sure you do if you're reading this book. Remember, momentum's primary component is direction. First, you must know where you want to go!

No Tactics = Circumstantial Suicide

Day 1: Alex runs 4 miles.
Day 2: Alex runs 4 miles.
Day 3: Alex doesn't run.
Day 4-17: Alex doesn't run.
Day 18: Alex runs 4 miles.
Days 19–92: Alex doesn't run.

What happened? Alex had direction! She wanted to run, perhaps for general health and fitness reasons. She aimed for four miles a day. But on day three, her ankle was sore. She couldn't run four miles. Unfortunately, she didn't even consider lower-impact cardio exercise or strength training as an alternative. Since she had no tactical answer to her change of circumstance, she did not generate any momentum on day three and for the next two weeks.

* * *

On day 18, she tried again, but quickly faded away for the same reason—she had no tactical answers when even minor obstacles arose. According to Sun Tzu's quote below, Alex is not a heaven-born captain (and who wouldn't want to be one of those?).

"Do not repeat the tactics which have gained you one victory, but let your methods be regulated by the infinite variety of circumstances. He who can modify his tactics in relation to his opponent and thereby succeed in winning may be called a heaven-born captain."
~ Sun Tzu

No Ability = Sure Defeat

Day 1: Alex plants the first seeds in her garden.
Day 5: It rained today. Instead of watering the plants as planned, Alex went shopping for more seeds and bought a gardening guidebook. Excellent tactical maneuvering!
Days 6–86: Alex neglects her plants.
Day 87: All of Alex's plants have been dead for a while now. In her words, *ain't nobody got time for dat!* Alex's busy schedule never gave her garden a chance—she didn't have the time needed to sustain a garden. She showed clear direction and impressive tactical maneuvering, but it never was a realistic goal.

Another example of no ability:

Day 1: Jon lifts weights as a part of his new fitness plan.

Day 8: Jon uses the one rest day he's allotted per month to recover from extreme soreness. Nice tactics, Jon!

Day 39: Jon really enjoys *Squid Game* on Netflix. He cried during the marble episode. Oh, what? Working out? No, Jon was trying an extreme workout program he didn't have the discipline to sustain. He was allowed only one rest day per month in the program, which wasn't enough. Since he couldn't sustain the brutal workouts for both disciplinary and physical reasons, he did the logical thing and quit.

Respect your limits. Better yet, aim well below your limits if sustainability is your goal (and it should be because of momentum!). Aiming below your maximum ability gives you a cushion in case you're wrong, allowing you to succeed, use tactics, and build higher. Since studies show that we overestimate our self-control ability, aiming lower than what every other self-help book tells you to do is the smarter choice.

It's *always* better to aim low, with the opportunity to crush your goal, than it is to aim too high and discourage, hurt, or even demoralize yourself if/when you fall short. I know this stands against 99% of self-help literature that tells you to get motivated and aim big. Real-world, consistent training beats romanticized notions of grandeur that sell books but don't help anyone. If you want to become great in any area, build a foundation first.

* * *

Golden nugget: Professionals train. Amateurs wish, hope, and shoot for the moon.

Variable Force and Rest: Why You Need to Stop Sometimes

To sustain momentum in a human life is not like sustaining momentum in physics. In physics, you want maximum force at all times in the proper direction to build and sustain the most momentum possible.

In a human life, momentum works best with periods of variable force followed by periods of variable rest. If you push yourself 100% all the time, not only will your momentum stop, but it will reverse.

It's counterintuitive, but rest and relaxation are a critical part of sustained momentum and success. It's best to think of it like a car. Cars can generate great momentum and sustain it for long periods of time. Can they do it indefinitely? No, they'll run out of gas eventually. Cars must come to a complete stop in order to fill the tank and continue forward.

Stop Glorifying "Grinding"

Some think people don't need rest, they just need to grind.

Sleep deprived? Just grind!
No vacation in six years? Way to grind!

Hate your life? That's the grind, baby!

It's almost a religion. Grinders grind, depriving themselves of rest, fun, and sleep for some vague idea of getting ahead because of their sacrifice. Sacrifice for the sake of sacrifice means nothing. I can sacrifice my gallbladder to a fictional god that I just made up. Where does that get me? Minus one gallbladder, I think.

Sacrificing sleep and sanity for money or results is better than giving your gallbladder to Rhodrogg, Gallbladder God of the Forest, but not much better if it costs you your health and well-being. I mean, one of the best ways to use money is to *improve* your health and well-being! So, we get this common life trajectory: wreck your health to make a lot of money and then use that money to (attempt to) get your health back. Health is easier to maintain than to regain. I digress.

Those who worship the grind (or Rhodrogg) will make sacrifices that are not only useless but counterproductive to their true desires.

Pushing yourself and working hard is not worthless. That's not what I'm saying. I'm saying that, if you make a sacrifice, you need to know the reason and true cost of it. While sleep deprivation and workaholism are trendy and cool these days, they carry a steep health, wellness, and productivity cost in the short and long term.

***

Occasionally, a poor night's sleep may be necessary to meet a deadline or capitalize on an opportunity, but, if it's a long-term situation, you're almost certainly making a mistake. No matter your situation, you will perform better with adequate sleep. Get it!

The reason people need varied rest and activity is that human energy is not fully predictable. Have you ever had food poisoning? Even when you aren't puking, it saps your energy because you can't eat. Beyond extreme situations like that, there are thousands of smaller forces that make our energy fluctuate daily. Respect those, and take a break when it's clear you need one.

Remember, we don't rest as a sign of weakness; we rest so that we can be at our strongest. If you disagree, wake up a hibernating bear and let *him* know your opinion about long naps and tell him that he's weak. My cats are basically small bears. They sleep a lot, of course, but, when they're active and playing, their energy level is best described as "nuclear."

Force Over Time: More Force is Not Always Better

Life is a fascinating juggling act because our results matter over all periods of time. We want a great minute, a great hour, a great week, a great three years, and a glorious life. All of the above. And yet, the optimal strategy to maximize the next five minutes (sprint) is absolutely different from the optimal strategy for the next month (moderate distance), which is different from the one for the next 15 years (marathon).

You can succeed spectacularly in a three-week period as you fail miserably over a three-month period. Many of us know this example through experience. New Year's Resolutions often play out this way. But why?

Your momentum source could only power you for three weeks. The method by which you succeeded those three weeks is the main reason you failed over three months.

Short-Term Success, Long-Term Failure
People think doing something for three weeks will create the momentum they need to succeed in the long term. If this were true, the people who attempt to transform their life overnight would turn into superheroes. But behavioral momentum doesn't work that way.

Three weeks of success is great! In terms of momentum, it means you've created momentum on 21 individual days, which together form a small amount of long-term momentum. That can and should increase your confidence, but you must retain a day-to-day mindset. The first 21 days of success will not and cannot "carry" day 22. If you believe they can, you will fail. If instead you recognize the need to create momentum on day 22 just as you did on day one, you will succeed.

Aiming high can kill your momentum, too. There are limits to how reliably you can create a high level of force over time. In the case of burnout, **your short-term success is your long-term failure**. They are the same. It's not that you started well and then didn't stick with it. It's that your strategy had almost no chance to succeed because it was degenerative.

The ideal momentum in a human life is similar to how a marathoner runs a race. It's best done at a pace you can create and sustain over all periods of time—now, later, and in 15 years. A sustainable pace matters more than how you perform in the first mile of the race.

What's most important in a marathon? Keep running.
What's most important for any goal or pursuit? Show up every day.

If you stop creating momentum, you lose. Choose your pace wisely! Or, better yet, don't leave it to chance and make it a sure thing by aiming lower than what you think you're capable of. This isn't settling for less, it's how you achieve more. Big accomplishments happen through consistent forward motion, not erratic jumps forwards and backwards.

Adjusting the Bar to Entry to Maximize Momentum

The higher the bar to entry, the fewer the entries. In economics, this concept creates monopolies. Without competitors, a monopolistic company can afford to stagnate and even price-gouge customers who have no other option.

Monopolies create a lousy situation for innovation, progress, consumers, and even the monopolistic business that is allowed to stagnate instead of being pushed to innovate by competitors. The same applies to personal development—a high bar to entry leads to personal stagnation because it deters attempts!

Who will make more progress?

- Open & Flexible: Person A will work out in any clothing, inside or outside (in any weather), at any time, and in any form. **Low bar to entry.**
- Closed & Rigid: Person B will only work out if it's Pilates in their sexy tiger-stripe shorts, indoors, and between 8 and 9 pm on a Wednesday with a full moon. **High bar to entry.**

Person A will have *significantly* more opportunities to exercise. The tiger-stripe shorts example is extreme and full of disturbing imagery—I apologize—but it reveals the principle. It's impossible for Person B to exercise consistently with such tiger- and moon-based requirements.

To be clear, working out in tiger-striped shorts during a full moon is absolutely going to result in the best workout of your life, for obvious reasons. But that's just one day. Generating too much power and speed initially is actually a mistake if you care about lasting success. Here's a real world example that is occurring as we speak:

- Person A will do one (or more) push-ups per day. Or more.
- Person B will do 100 push-ups (or more) per day. No fewer.

The 100 push-up challenge exists and is quite popular. I've written *Mini Habits*, which is about doing one push-up a day (among other small habits).

Both concepts deal with daily push-ups. People have succeeded with both methods, too, so it's more of a question of efficiency and reliability. Which method is most likely to result in success for most people?

It depends on what time frame you look at. At what point do we measure success? The first day? Week? Month? 10 years from now?

Doing 100 push-ups a day is fantastic exercise if you can do it. If you did it every day for 30 years, it would clearly be the superior method if exercise is your goal, as it theoretically produces 100x more exercise than a one-push-up goal. The only problem is the high chance of long-term failure.

People commonly aim to do the 100 push-up challenge for 30 days or something similar. By the end of the challenge, the person is likely to be mentally and physically fatigued from forcing this static level of exertion daily. With such a strict goal, no tactics or variability are even allowed. Remember the analogy of the car running out of gas? This goal doesn't allow for pit stops *or* turbo boosts.

One push-up or more a day generates a small amount of momentum every day, but the momentum is accumulative instead of degenerative. The ask is so small that it can even act as a rest day, while still keeping your momentum and winning streak alive. Importantly, the one push-up acts as a floor (starting point) rather than a ceiling (ending point) as in the 100 push-up challenge. If you're already in push-up position, it's easy to use the momentum from your first push-up to do more of them.

I've actually tried both challenges. I think I lasted three days in the 100 push-up challenge. I know that's lame, but that's why I need better strategies. If you were to measure success at day three, the 100 push-up challenge would be 100x better than the one push-up challenge for me. But what happens after day three?

* * *

I currently do full workouts nearly every day solely because of that one push-up *nine years ago*. I mean that literally, too. I did not work out consistently before that single push-up I did in late 2012. Here I am, nine years later, with a new relationship with exercise. That's the power of an accumulative momentum strategy. It still blows my mind every day how I got here.

Day 3: The 100 push-up challenge is 100x better on the third day (probably less, because the one-push-up challenge doesn't end with one push-up, but begins with it.)

Year 9: The one-push-up challenge is *infinitely better*. The 100 push-up challenge doesn't last this long except in extremely rare cases. The one-push-up challenge results in a new relationship with exercise and robust daily workouts.

Earlier, you may remember I said, "The method by which we succeeded those three weeks is the main reason we failed over three months." In the same way, the method by which some would say I "failed" by only doing a few measly push-ups a day is the primary reason I've succeeded over nine years.

If the aim is to gain momentum, and it should be, you must be able to overcome the variable resistance you face

every day.

The superiority of smaller, lower-effort steps over big, high-effort steps is a predictable outcome based on what we know about human psychology and neuroscience. Small steps forward can accumulate momentum over time, whereas sweeping changes start strong and appear to have momentum but are quickly rejected and aggressively slowed by the subconscious brain, almost always reverting to the mean (where they started).

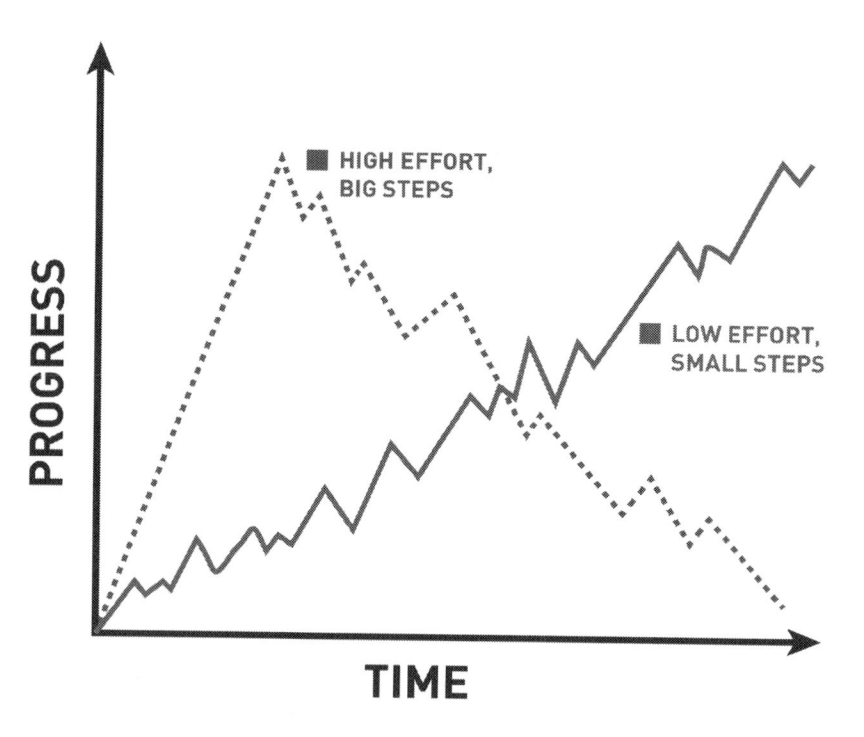

This graph shows different books' ideas about how to succeed. Depending on when you look at results, you will end up with a different "most successful" strategy. At the beginning or even mid-term, people will wonder why anyone would ever go small when they can get much better results with a bigger effort right now. Over time, the story changes.

The rapid start of an overly ambitious goal presents an unsustainable trajectory, and, just like any financial asset that's ever been on an unsustainable trajectory, the only direction to go is down. Life's roughly 28,000 days play out more like a marathon than a sprint, and which marathoners go for a 100% sprint at the very beginning of the race? The ones who lose or don't finish!

The smartest marathoners (and people) find a pace well below what they think they can sustain for the entire race. In a long race, it's better to be too conservative than to overshoot your ability and burn out before the end. **If you're conservative in your planning, you can use extra energy as it becomes clear that you can afford it.**

Momentum and Power: Not Always What They Seem

Early in the book, I mentioned that a fired bullet has more momentum than pollen in the wind. What if I told you that pollen in the wind actually has more momentum than a fired bullet most of the time?

Of course pollen has less momentum than a fired bullet

initially, but it doesn't end there. A bullet will travel about one mile in seconds, but then it stops completely. Meanwhile, pollen keeps going. Genetically modified grass pollen has been found in grasses over 13 miles away.[1] And if you think that's impressive, pine pollen has been found as high as 2,000 feet in the air and can travel up to 1,800 miles![2]

As a fired bullet lies motionless on the ground, pollen remains active in the air. Thus, the pollen actually has more momentum for all but a few seconds of time. The lightweight nature of pollen enables it to benefit from the power of the wind as it escapes gravity, while the bullet falls quickly.

Momentum over time seems counterintuitive to the human mind. How strange that one push-up can beat 100 and the statement "pollen has more momentum than a fired bullet" is true for all but a few seconds of time. The power and short-term momentum of a bullet embarrasses the floating piece of pollen for those first moments, and yet, it is the pollen that remains in motion for much longer, sometimes going more than 1000x the distance of the bullet. I implore you to always look beyond the initial impact of a considered action.

Golden (pollen) nugget: We shouldn't be so quick to judge the power and meaning of an action by its size or immediate result.

The Magic of Momentum

* * *

"The gentle overcomes the rigid.
The slow overcomes the fast.
The weak overcomes the strong.

Everyone knows that the yielding overcomes the stiff,
and the soft overcomes the hard.
Yet no one applies this knowledge."
~ Lao Tzu

Dear Lao, we're trying!

We've said that, to sustain momentum, you must embrace variable periods of rest and action and prioritize small forward steps over large (unsustainable) leaps. Just because you can do something bigger does not mean it's better... it may even be worse! I've experienced this many times when I overexert myself in a workout and end up too sore or injured to work out for the next several days. If I had taken it easier, I could have exercised *more* over time!

Momentum is magical because it compounds. This is so exciting for our lives because it means we are closer to our goals and dreams than we think we are! If you think about a goal in terms of incremental steps, it may seem far away and highly difficult. But if you could see what it looked like in a positive momentum vortex, it would seem a lot closer, doable, and enticing.

* * *

The Final Lesson: This Defeats Resistance Every Time

Bookmark this, highlight it, print it out, or tape it on your brother's forehead. Do whatever you need to do to remember this, because it works. This is the grand finale of the book.

Momentum comes from action.

Wherever we take an action, we generate motion in a specific direction—that translates to immediate short-term momentum in that area and related areas. Long-term momentum is the power we all desire, but consistently created short-term momentum is the only way to get there. So it comes down to this: we need to know how to take action.

When we want to take action and have the energy to do it, there's no problem. We do the action and improve our day and life. This is called being motivated, and it's very nice but not inevitable or reliable. We need to get to a point where motivation is irrelevant. We need to know how to be unstoppable.

To experience the magic of momentum, you must know how to beat resistance. It is the only thing that stops a person from taking action. It comes in many forms—excuses, low energy, busyness, emotions, procrastination, doubt, perfectionism, and so on. You can read the best, most motivating, smartest advice in the world. You will still face resistance. *You will struggle to take the right action sometimes.* This is the human condition! But read the following carefully and you won't be stopped anymore.

When you face resistance to action, you have two moves.

1. Overcome the resistance through brute force of will.
2. Consider an alternate action.

Most everyone tries option #1. It can work, but there are concrete downsides to it, the main ones being fatigue and failure. It takes a lot of energy to force an action you resist. You are literally fighting yourself, which is as exhausting as it sounds. Some studies suggest a forced action now can cause lower willpower later too. Resist now, cave into temptation (or inaction) later. Other studies have found that willpower is belief-based, meaning those who believe they have it have it. Personally, I think it's a combination of each of these.

Those who believe in their power to overcome resistance will certainly have greater success than those who don't. That's the role of belief. But we also operate in an energy-dependent and stress-sensitive body, meaning that real depletion occurs as we make decisions. You can push your limits mentally just as you can physically, but, as pushing your limits physically may cause injury, pushing your limits mentally may cause a breakdown.

* * *

With the willpower way, you may succeed for some time until your energy gets so depleted and your cortisol levels so high that you simply can't continue physically and/or mentally. In fact, we already know this happens because we have a name for it—burnout.

The strongest people can push themselves so hard that their minds and/or bodies quit on them, rendering them weak. The smartest people don't let that happen. The smarter you are, the better you can use your strength.

The tricky thing about this process is that you will appear somewhat invincible to yourself and/or others... until the moment of breakdown. On a less extreme level, we see people fail to continue with goals all the time. Most people quit before burnout, which is the smart move.

If you experience true burnout, not only will you be unable to make the progress you're striving for but it may also force you to take an extended break. Human beings pay for burnout with time.

But wait, there's also that second move, and we should consider it! When I say "alternate action," I don't mean changing from running a marathon to eating nachos. That new action doesn't align with your original vision, so, while there's less resistance to it, it also won't help you. Rather, your alternate action should be of the same type, just an easier, less intimidating version of it.

Why People Resist Easy Actions (and the Permanent Fix)

Easy actions offer a low-energy cost and non-threatening commitment level. So how could anyone *resist* such an easy win? People resist difficult actions because they are a known and overwhelming quantity of *work*. People will resist doing something easier as an alternative for three *philosophical* reasons.

1. It looks like **conceding defeat**. You wanted the big prize/success/marathon, and now you're settling for so much less.
2. It doesn't seem **significant enough** to matter.
3. We want to feel strong, and retreating to something easier makes us **feel weak**.

We want to win. We want to make significant progress. We want to be and feel strong. Okay. That's understandable psychology, but let's look at these points to see if they hold up under scrutiny. Unlike effort- and work-based resistance to action, a change in perspective alone can conquer philosophical resistance.

It's worth it to fine-tune your perspective of smaller actions because it will release an avalanche of positive momentum opportunities in your life. This is *the* key to overcoming resistance to action. This is *the* way to leverage the power of momentum and change your life.

Conceding Defeat? Actually, the Opposite!

This one looks logical at first glance but falls apart the moment you look closely. To explain why, let me ask you something. What does it mean to concede defeat? What does waving the white flag suggest will happen next?

Universally, when someone concedes defeat, it means they will not make another move forward and will not attack again. For example, in chess, conceding means no more moves are played and your opponent wins. In any sort of combat, the conceding person or army remains still in a non-threatening position. No advance of any kind is done when conceding defeat.

We used the example of running earlier, so what would a defeated runner do? That's simple. A defeated runner wouldn't run at all. And therein lies our answer. Running unimpressively *is still running*. It's active. What warrior, while still fighting, can be said to be defeated?

Doing less of something is not a concession of defeat; in fact, it can be part of an effective attack. A boxer wants his opponent to laugh at jabs, because they set up the devastating hook.

In my favorite movie, *Gladiator* (movie spoilers ahead), the villain, Commodus, secretly stabs the main character,

Maximus, with a knife in his back just before they face mortal combat in the Colosseum. Then he tells his people to "conceal the wound." This cowardly move all but ensures that Maximus will be an ineffective fighter and will die soon, without the crowd knowing Commodus cheated him out of a fair fight.

This scene makes me cry. The hero's inevitable death is sad, but most of my tears result from what he does *after* this moment. Maximus *never* concedes defeat. That hits deep. I don't just feel sad for Maximus in this moment; I'm proud of him. He's showing courage, determination, and the human spirit to fight.

Maximus, weak from blood loss, will not fight well. He can barely move. He's hallucinating. The pain is excruciating. He's going to die soon. Stumbling, he fights the best that he can. *This is what it means to never concede defeat.*

I have a question for you, and I want you to think about it sincerely. Why do we honor and respect heroic characters like Maximus for fighting the best he can when he's hurting and yet berate ourselves for doing the same? Why do we see Maximus's actions as brave but anything similar from ourselves as pathetic? This isn't just unfair; it actively deters greatness. It prevents us from becoming the heroes and victors of our own stories.

Everyone has pain in their lives. Everyone is wounded.

Nobody is invincible. This doesn't disqualify us from glory, honor, or even the chance of victory. Every day, you have the opportunity to show your merit.

It is when we are weak, tired, or out of energy that we fight *tactically*. We may not ever be at full strength, and we may not do all that we hoped to accomplish today, but our unimpressive effort to move forward remains the very opposite of conceding defeat; it is not shameful, sad, or worthless, it is meaningful and inspiring, just as it was for Maximus!

So, the next time you think of doing something small as conceding defeat, picture the heroic Maximus, mortally wounded, crippled, hallucinating from blood loss; picture him barely able to walk, staggering out to the battlefield (to the epic score of Gladiator). This is what a hero looks like. Maximus could not fight a tenth as well as he wanted, *but he still fought.*

Doing less than you originally intended or less than you deem ideal does not mean you're giving up. It means the exact opposite—you're a warrior who will fight for every inch of progress you can get.

Not Significant Enough to Matter? More Significant than Anything!

I could refer you to the entire book for this one. But this is such a common miscalculation that it deserves a revisit.

Promise yourself that you will never again consider only the immediate result of an action. Consider the infinite ripples that emanate from it! Consider the meaning of a small step forward when you would otherwise do nothing. Calculate the result of repeatedly deciding to move forward instead of backward over your lifetime. It's impossible to calculate but we know it's good!

In the same way I admit I can't fathom the size and speed of a hypervelocity star, I cannot fathom the chain reactions and total momentum of even one positive action. Maximus says in Gladiator (the Marcus Aurelius quote), "What we do in life echoes in eternity."

Retreating is Weak? Not Always.
We wanted the five-mile run today. Or the marathon. Or some other arbitrary milestone. But now we're retreating to one measly run around the block. Is that weakness?

In warfare, retreating is sometimes the response to losing a battle, but not always. An army can retreat to higher ground or another terrain that is easier to defend. They may retreat to lead the opposing forces into an ambush. Armies may even retreat to feign weakness and give the enemy a false sense of superiority and comfort, only to attack shortly thereafter. Retreating is far more tactical, strong, and useful than the simple "you won and now I'm gonna run away" image it has.

* * *

If you play chess, you know that there are times to retreat and times to attack. If your opponent moves their pawn, protected by another pawn, into an attacking position against your queen, you must move her to safety! It's not weak to do so; it's smart to protect your most valuable piece and move it to a more favorable spot.

In life, we will face many moments where the "plan" we had in mind is untenable. These are times to step back, to retreat. Our retreat, however, isn't like a weak-willed soldier in a war movie; it is like a chess grandmaster protecting the queen, which will later win the game. Also consider that a skilled chess player may retreat the queen but do so to a square that *counterattacks* the opponent or sets the other pieces up for an attack later in the game.

Now that we've covered each of these points of philosophical resistance, consider once more the idea of doing *less* of something that you resist doing. Especially consider this idea against the alternatives, which are doing nothing or forcing the full action (which is useful at times but exhausting and unsustainable).

1. A small attack is still an active attack; not concession, but progression!
2. A small attack can stack, Jack. Stacked attacks crack backs, Shaq. I don't know why I'm suddenly trying to rap. I'm trying to say that momentum (easily generated from small attacks) is *exponential*, not linear. That's genuine

power.

3. Though it may be a "retreat" from a previously bigger aim, remember that retreating in this way is a tactical move done to **strengthen** your position. When you can turn a certain loss into a small win that carries momentum, that's certainly strengthening!

Every time in your life you don't feel like doing the thing that you know would improve your life (now and later), think of this. Don't fall into the all-or-nothing trap. Don't believe the people who say "go big or go home." Don't concede defeat because you're hurt. Don't sit out just because you're not at your best. Grit your teeth and move forward today, even if you end up crawling when you wanted to run. If you take these words to heart, you will be basically unstoppable. Resistance has no chance against a cunning, resilient tactician!

When You Carry Full Momentum

The change from sporadic momentum to full, consistent momentum is revelatory. Momentum is a free resource—we just need to use the proper tools to access it and gain its full power.

Almost everyone would like to change their lives for the better. What if they tried to change their day instead? You can change the entire texture of your day with one small action because of the momentum it generates. We've all experienced this for better and worse, haven't we? Maybe a deep meditation session has single-handedly made your day before. On the flip side, maybe an argument or poor choice has ruined your day. That's momentum. Every day, it determines your trajectory behind the scenes.

You can't live weeks, months, or years at a time. You live one day at a time. Thus, those who master how to live a day also master how to live a life.

Every moment of every day is a chance to create momentum, life's most powerful force. If you feel stuck, revisit these final chapters for specific strategies to get moving. Or reread the entire book if you ever forget the incredible power you wield as someone who can create positive momentum.

Thank you so much for reading *The Magic of Momentum*. Onward!

Cheers,
Stephen Guise

Thank You!

You've given me the greatest gift you can give an author. You read my book! It means the world to me. Thank you.

The next best gift you can give an author is to write a review. Would you tell others what you thought about this book by leaving a quick review on Amazon? It doesn't have to be fancy or long. Reviews are more important to me than most because I'm an independent author. Thank you for considering it.

The Magic of Momentum Book Page: minihabits.com/momentum
Website: stephenguise.com
Email: sguise@deepexistence.com

Other Books by Stephen

Mini Habits
My first book! This is the book that started the small habits craze that has taken over the publishing industry in the last decade. It's a worldwide bestseller in 21 languages and people love it. I also made it into a video course, which has over 20,000 students!

Book: amazon.com/dp/B00HGKNBDK
Video Course: udemy.com/course/mini-habit-mastery/

Mini Habits for Weight Loss
Diets have been shown to make you gain weight, even more than not dieting. Instead, try this habit-driven approach to weight loss, and your changes can last.

Book: amazon.com/dp/B01N0FR4AX
Video Course: udemy.com/course/weight-loss-mini-habits/

How to Be an Imperfectionist (Book)
This book applies *Mini Habits* to the problem of perfectionism. If you struggle with depression, fear, and inaction, this book has a lot to offer.

Book: amazon.com/dp/B00UMG535Y

Elastic Habits **(Book)**
This is *Mini Habits* with a twist! Instead of just having a small daily goal, elastic habits give you the option for mini (easy), plus (medium), and elite (hard) wins every day. Some days are better than others, and an elastic habit can adapt to the unique texture of each day.

Book: www.amazon.com/dp/B08188WBGC

Tuesday Messages
Every Tuesday, I write to subscribers. People have told me this content is life-changing.
Sign up: stephenguise.com/subscribe/

Why This Book?

[1] There are 100 senators in the United States, and 37% of USA presidents to date have been selected from this pool of people. The odds still aren't great, but they are significantly higher than those of any other group of people.

Introduction: Momentum Isn't Fair

[1] After the meet was over, the swimming officials discussed what happened in a top-secret meeting. Since we didn't break any swim meet rules at the time, they decided to count our win. For obvious reasons, however, they would not allow our exploit in future meets. (Lifeguard: "WALK!")

[2] The Oxford English Dictionary | Oxford Languages (2022). Retrieved 6 March 2022, from https://languages.oup.com/research/oxford-english-dictionary/

[3] Permutt, S. (2011). The Efficacy of Momentum-Stopping Timeouts on Short-Term Performance in the National Basketball Association. Retrieved 6 March 2022, from https://scholarship.tricolib.brynmawr.edu/bitstream/handle/10066/6918/2011PermuttS_thesis.pdf

★ ★ ★

The Magic of Momentum

1. 1903 – The First Flight – Wright Brothers National Memorial (2015). Retrieved 6 March 2022, from https://www.nps.gov/wrbr/learn/historyculture/thefirstflight.htm
2. Napiwotzki, R., & Heber, U. (2005). Star on the run. Retrieved 6 March 2022, from https://www.eso.org/public/news/eso0536/
3. The Quetzalcoatlus dinosaur was thought to weigh about 500 pounds, with a 40-foot wingspan, but nobody thinks about Quetzalcoatlus dinosaurs.

Principle 1

1. This can also be called inertia, which is defined as "a tendency to do nothing or remain unchanged" (The Oxford English Dictionary). If you're doing nothing, you're most likely to continue doing nothing. If you're doing something, you're most likely to keep doing that same thing.
2. If this sounds familiar, I was the first to use Newton's Law of Motion as a metaphor for personal development in my book *Mini Habits* (2013).

Principle 2

1. The basal ganglia have an easy job, because all they do is repeat patterns that result in reward (pleasure, success, satisfaction, etc.). The prefrontal cortex has a tougher job. It's concerned with both short and long term, and it must weigh the risk and reward of behaviors across all spectrums of time. When you consider a good ol' toilet scrubbing and your brain says "NO!", that's your immediate subconscious preference talking. You know from experience that toilet cleaning isn't fun. But your prefrontal cortex brought up the idea because it sees two potential futures:

1. Sparkling clean toilet
2. Microorganism dance rave

The prefrontal cortex can understand that cleaning the toilet, while not fun now, is a lot more fun later. It can also decide not to have that extra drink or to plan the day intentionally instead of floating along aimlessly. If that sounds like a lot of work, well, of course it is! That's why the energy-intensive prefrontal cortex is not the whole of our brain, which is necessarily designed for both energy efficiency and power.

2. Roughly 21 to 29 percent of patients prescribed opioids for chronic pain misuse them.

Between 8 and 12 percent of people using an opioid for chronic pain develop an opioid use disorder.

An estimated 4 to 6 percent who misuse prescription opioids transition to heroin.

About 80 percent of people who use heroin first misused prescription opioids.

Likelihood of developing an opioid use disorder depends on many factors, including length of time a person is prescribed to take opioids for acute pain and length of time that people continue taking opioids (whether as prescribed or misused).

Source: National Institute on Drug Abuse. 2021. Opioid Overdose Crisis | National Institute on Drug Abuse. [online] Available at: <https://nida.nih.gov/drug-topics/opioids/opioid-overdose-crisis>

[3] To those of you who just suggested that I sprinkle cocaine over the broccoli, that... could work, but then I wouldn't really be addicted to the broccoli, would I? The problem with such strategies is that avoiding cocaine is more important than eating broccoli. I'm sure that I could develop a broccoli addiction this way, but it might also be a cocaine addiction. I'm doing just fine with my broccoli intake, but I appreciate your concern and know you were just trying to help.

NOTE: I've never tried cocaine on broccoli or otherwise. I am terrified of trying any hard drug even one time. That's what happens when you study neuroscience!

[4] I'm not one to say that people shouldn't have vices or guilty pleasures. I've got them, and I enjoy them. But people don't read books about how to increase their love of chocolate, because that's effortless. Instead of pitting vices against "healthy" behaviors, we can instead highlight the real goal—control and mastery. We want to design our lifestyles, not be tossed around in the chaotic sea of impulse and choice.

[5] The first successful parachute jump was actually made by André-Jacques Garnerin from a hydrogen balloon, 3,200 feet above Paris, way back in 1797. Imagine being the first person to try that!

Source: How Was Skydiving Invented? (2018). Retrieved 6 March 2022, from https://www.skydivecoastalcarolinas.com/blog/how-was-skydiving-invented/

[6] Is Skydiving Worth It? | Skydiving NYC | Skydive Long Island. (2016). Retrieved 6 March 2022, from https://www.skydivelongisland.com/about/articles/is-skydiving-worth-it/

* * *

Principle 3

1. The exact length of time it takes to form a habit is a very complicated question. How big is the habit? How many reps of the habit are you doing per day? How much do you like the habit? We don't really know precisely how long it takes to form a habit, but we do know it's like building a muscle. You don't work on building a muscle and then suddenly have one after 27 days. You start out with weak muscles and work on them to grow stronger and stronger. It's a spectrum of progress, not a destination. Habits are the same way, a spectrum of behavioral preferences of variable strengths. We have strong habits and weak habits.

2. To best understand why behaviors are still weak after 30 days without much momentum, consider that you've already established most of your other habits over years or decades. Habits compete with one another for your attention and energy, and the habits you hope to replace are still stronger than the new one after 30 days. But remember, that's only scary if your habit formation strategy doesn't extend beyond 30 days. Let's look at an example.

What you do the first thing in the morning, immediately upon waking up? If you're like me, you roll over and look at your phone for way too long. (I know, this whole book is invalid now because I publicly admitted to having a bad habit.) That habit is tied to an even more robust, broader habit of all the other times you look at your phone.

For many people, looking at their phone is a multi-cue habit they've built through dozens of repetitions a day for many years. And you think that doing yoga in the morning for 30 days can compete with it? Ha!

3. Ballard, C. (2014). Kobe Bryant on growing old, Dwight Howard and his inner Zen. Retrieved 6 March 2022, from https://www.si.com/nba/2014/08/26/kobe-bryant-lakers-dwight-howard-tony-allen-retirement

4. Lally, P., van Jaarsveld, C. H. M., Potts, H. W. W., & Wardle, J. How are habits formed: Modelling habit formation in the real world. Eur. J. Soc. Psychol. (2010), vol. 40, 998–1009. doi: 10.1002/ejsp.674

5. It didn't take nine years for me to "get results." After about a year, I had established a good workout routine. Nine years later, my fitness routines and goals are more advanced and easier to pursue.

6. In a rut (phrase): "kept in an established way of living or working that never changes."

source: "in a rut" (n.d.) McGraw-Hill Dictionary of American Idioms and Phrasal Verbs (2002). Retrieved March 31 2022, from https://

idioms.thefreedictionary.com/in+a+rut

Principle 4

[1] As someone who gambles and invests, I'm acutely familiar with both of these! Gambling is a guaranteed loss in the long run, but people still do it for that chance of a short-term win. That immediate impact of winning feels great. Investing, if done smartly, is a guaranteed win in the long term, but the immediate impact of investing is almost nonexistent. It's not a rush to see your holding move up fractions of a percent each day. But over time, your gains can compound and create a fortune. In both cases, we're better off considering the longer-term result over the short-term result.

[2] Attia, P. (2012). Do calories matter? The Eating Academy. Retrieved 30 August 2016, from http://eatingacademy.com/nutrition/do-calories-matter

[3] Strapagiel, L., 2017. This Guy Helped Save A Life By Paying It Forward At The Tim Hortons Drive Thru. [online] BuzzFeed. Available at: <https://www.buzzfeed.com/laurenstrapagiel/this-guy-saved-a-life-by-paying-it-forward-at-the-tim>

[4] Spada, F. (2016). Fearless [Image]. Retrieved from https://flickr.com/photos/lfphotos/31580887472/in/photolist-Q7GizS-ZEcJBm

[5] You know how the stereotype is that cruises and Florida are for old people? I live in Florida and I've been on more than 10 cruises. I'm 36, and my 16-year-old niece thinks I'm old. The other day, she said that we come from "very different generations." That comment aged me 15 years.

Chapter 5

[1] Bennett, G., Foley, P., Levine, E., Whiteley, J., Askew, S., & Steinberg, D., et al. (2013). Behavioral treatment for weight gain prevention among Black women in primary care practice. JAMA Internal Medicine, 173(19), 1770. http://dx.doi.org/10.1001/jamainternmed.2013.9263

[2] This makes me think of the scene in first The Lord of the Rings movie in which the orc captain Lurtz battles with the fellowship. This orc was literally bred to fight, and you can see it when Strider stabs him. Most people and orcs react negatively when stabbed in the gut. But Lurtz, the crazy orc, grabs the knife, smiles, and licks the blood off of it. He loves warfare as much as man flesh! He loves warfare so much that he seemed to enjoy getting stabbed. That gives him an advantage over anyone who only fights out of necessity, because he's willing to go farther, be more aggressive, fight to the death, and still rate the experience 5 stars on Yelp. When you do something long enough, you become more like Lurtz, in which situations that would typically be uncomfortable are now enjoyable.

[3] As I said in Mini Habits for Weight Loss, those who go on diets put far more effort into their dietary and movement choices than everyone else, and studies show they get worse results than even non-dieters. Yikes! Dieting burns you out and gives you no (long-term) results. It's a classic example of the inequality of effort, momentum, and results.

Significant calorie restriction is anti-momentum biologically (by inducing the starvation response) and psychologically (it's a difficult, short-term aim). Dieters put forth superhuman effort. People love food, and dieters semi-starve themselves! I don't know how they do it, honestly, but again, momentum matters more than effort, so that effort is unfortunately wasted.

[4] Cuddy, A. (2012). Your body language may shape who you are [Video]. Retrieved from https://www.ted.com/talks/amy_cuddy_your_body_language_may_shape_who_you_are?language=en

Manipulation vs Control

[1] Retrieved 6 March 2022, from https://www.merriam-webster.com/dictionary/manipulation

Chapter 7

[1] Lubin, R. (2017). New study reveals how much you'll spend on sandwiches over your lifetime. Retrieved 6 March 2022, from https://www.mirror.co.uk/news/uk-news/sandwich-again-new-poll-says-10116627

[2] Sato, S., Yoshida, R., Murakoshi, F., Sasaki, Y., Yahata, K., Nosaka, K., & Nakamura, M. (2022). Effect of daily 3-second maximum voluntary isometric, concentric, or eccentric contraction on elbow flexor strength. Scandinavian Journal of Medicine & Science in Sports. doi: 10.1111/sms.14138

[3] To be clear, this is a different technique than Mel Robbins's "5-second rule," in which you count down from five and then begin an action… although that's also a great technique to try and can be combined with this one. The seven-second spark technique is about your initial commitment.

[4] Cuddy, A. (2012). Your body language may shape who you are [Video]. Retrieved from https://www.ted.com/talks/amy_cuddy_your_body_language_may_shape_who_you_are?language=en

* * *

Chapter 8

[1] Monroe, D. (2004). GM Pollen Spreads Much Farther Than Previously Thought. Retrieved 6 March 2022, from https://www.scientificamerican.com/article/gm-pollen-spreads-much-fa/

[2] Gone with the wind: Far-flung pine pollen still potent miles from the tree. (2010). Retrieved 6 March 2022, from https://www.eurekalert.org/news-releases/755801

Made in the USA
Columbia, SC
23 April 2025